THE

Collected

Written by

Michael O'Neill & Carolyn Thomas

Danann
BOOKS

© Danann Publishing Limited 2019

First Published Danann Publishing Ltd 2019

WARNING: For private domestic use only, any unauthorised Copying, hiring,
lending or public performance of this book is illegal.

CAT NO: DAN0448

Photography courtesy of

Getty images

Hulton Archive

Michael Ochs Archives / Stringer

Keystone / Stringer

Popperfoto

GAB Archive / Redferns

Keystone

Juergen Vollmer/Redferns

Keystone Features / Stringer

Horst Fascher/K & K Ulf Kruger OHG/Redferns

Paul Popper/Popperfoto

Bettmann

Rolls Press/Popperfoto

Ralph Morse/The LIFE Picture Collection

Movie Poster Image Art

Santi Visalli

Express / Stringer

Cummings Archives/Redferns

David Redfern/Redferns

Mondadori Portfolio

Evening Standard/Getty Images

Express / Stringer

Ron Galella/WireImage

RB/Redferns

Ron Howard/Redferns

Bill Ray/The LIFE Picture Collection

Estate Of Keith Morris/Redferns

CBS Photo Archive

Central Press

Max Scheler - K & K/Redferns

Sunday Mirror/Mirrorpix/Mirrorpix

LMPC

Mark and Colleen Hayward/Redferns

Other images - Wikimedia Commons

Book layout & design Darren Grice at Ctrl-d

Copy Editor Juliette O'Neill

All rights reserved. No Part of this title may be reproduced or transmitted in any material form (including
photocopying or storing it in any medium by electronic means and whether or not transiently or
incidentally to some other use of this publication) without the written permission of the copyright owner,
except in accordance with the provisions of the Copyright, Designs and Patents Act 1988.Applications for
the copyright owner's written permission should be addressed to the publisher.

Made in EU.

ISBN: 978-1-912332-41-0

CONTENTS

LIVERPOOL DRAINPIPES

Mention the year 1940 to any ardent Beatles fan and the chances are they will not have images of Luftwaffe bombs falling on Liverpool docks and the River Mersey coursing past their inner eye. But what probably will happen is that two dates will automatically be conjured up from their heavily stocked archives of Beatles' miscellanea, swiftly followed by two more. The magical dates? The 7th of July 1940; the 9th of October 1940; the 18th of June 1942; the 25th of February 1943.

Yes, what else could they be but the dates of birth for Ringo Starr, John Lennon, Paul McCartney and George Harrison, whose lucky stars brought them together and made them "more popular than Jesus". Let's be fair, though, the four Scousers did have an advantage; Jesus didn't play guitar, as far as we know.

A few years had to pass before these four dates would mean anything to anybody, except some very proud parents, and a few not so proud, so let's pick them off one by one and trace the long and winding road to stardom for each of the Fab Four.

In July 1940, Ringo Starr was not christened. Not christened Ringo, that is. As the water drops fell on his noddle on July the 28th, he was named Richard, son of Elsie and Richard Starkey. Richard junior's young years were slightly more dramatic than those of his future bandmate John, but like him, his father featured but little in his life, preferring the pub and alcoholic dreaming to his new son. Ringo's mother worked in a bar to make ends meet, so little Richie, as he was nicknamed, spent a lot of time with his grandfather, seemingly content with a solitary life. His parents finally divorced in 1945.

And then, when he was 6, Ritchie was struck down with appendicitis, which then developed into peritonitis; it almost killed him, putting him into a coma for several weeks. Most of the following year he spent in hospital, only returning home in May 1948. Having lost ground dramatically at school, unable to read or write, it took him until 1953 to catch up – at which point he contracted tuberculosis. This time he was placed in a sanatorium for two years.

And yet; his stay sowed the seeds of his future success, because he was encouraged to join the hospital band, and it was at that point – wielding a makeshift cotton bobbin mallet and hammering away at the cabinets beside his bed – that his unshakable love for percussion was born.

An academic career having been sabotaged by his health, Richard Starkey Jr. left St. Silas Church of England primary school and, ineligible for the eleven plus exam, moved on to Dingle Vale Secondary Modern School.

The next important step forward in his unusual progress, however, arrived in the shape of Harry Graves, whom his mother married in 1953 when Richie was almost 13. It was a happy partnership for young Richard, who found unexpected gentleness and a warm relationship with his stepfather. And there was one other very important fact about Harry Graves; he adored big bands and filled his new young protégé's ears with the likes of Dinah Shore and Billy Daniels.

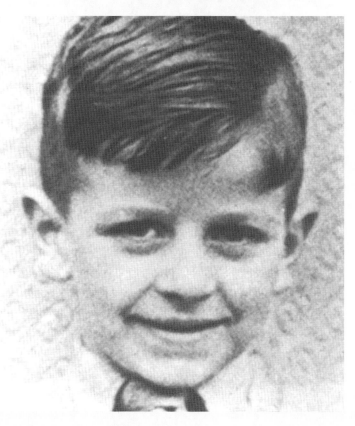

Clockwise from top left: Paul, George, John and Ringo

There was to be no more school life for Richard Starkey following his illnesses. He stayed at home, listening to music and beating out rhythms. And then came work, which he needed so that he could buy warm clothes to stave off more illness in the damp and cold house. He tried his hand at being a waiter on a boat and had a brief stint as a railway worker; but failing a physical examination, he was released and had to manage on welfare.

It was Harry who stepped in to help. He found Richard an apprenticeship as a machinist with an equipment manufacturer. And there Ritchie became friends with Roy Trafford... and Roy loved skiffle. Oh yes. Soon, Ritchie did, too.

It was 1956. Roy and Richard began to sing together, and before long they were joined by a guitar-playing neighbour of Richard's, Eddie Miles. The three then formed the Eddie Miles Band, which morphed into Eddie Clayton and the Clayton Squares.

Such was Richard's prowess that in 1959 he was playing for a group known as the Ravin Texans, afterwards renamed the Hurricanes, the backing group for the singer Roy Storm; a very successful partnership. Richie became Rings, of which he wore a lot, and then Ringo; it sounded more wild west.

One Beatle was up and drumming.

Meanwhile, in another area of Liverpool...

Picture now those Luftwaffe bombs raining down from the sky over Liverpool and John Winston Lennon (in honour of Winston Churchill) barely 20 minutes old, when a landmine falling directly outside the hospital where he was born almost allowed Jesus to remain the most popular person in the world.

But little John survived. Nonetheless, he presented a slight problem for his mother Julia when she met a new man friend - Julia's husband, Freddie Lennon, had soon disappeared from her life; within a few years of their marriage in 1938, in fact. But Julia's sister, Mimi, (having prodded the social services) had no hesitation in accepting the rather unwanted baby - although Julia visited every day, as Mimi lived not far away.

And so it was that John went to live with Mimi and her husband George in a bourgeois, semi-detached house in the leafy village of Woolton just outside Liverpool. Even at the height of his fame, John would telephone her every week, until his murder in 1980.

Remember Penny Lane? It was very close to John's first school, Dovedale Primary where, by all accounts, John was a precociously able student, despite the discovery that his eyesight was bad. Even at that age he loved writing and loved reading, and his strong character would brook no nonsense. Rebel or not, he could be found singing in the choir at St Peter's Church in Woolton, although he would become known for his antics and mischievousness. And not just in church.

As he grew older, the leader of his four-pack of friends, his fearlessness led him into rather more serious anti-social behaviour; smashing street lamps, throwing clumps of earth at trains and shoplifting. Lots of shoplifting. And he continued his shoplifting career through to the age of 12, when he began to cycle the mile or so to his new school; Quarry Bank Grammar.

It wasn't an illustrious career there. Aided and abetted by his best friend from primary school, Pete Shotton, Lennon began a not so slow slide from top of the class into the dungeon, with canings to help him along.

Barely had he begun his new school when George died. The man who had been John's ally and friend could no longer exert a benevolent influence on the boy who was now wallowing in his own world free from schoolwork and rules, propped up by insolence, betting and skiving off school. There would be little that Mimi could do to restrain the fatherless boy.

10

What now did he feel when he visited his mother Julia, from whom, it seemed, he had inherited his devil-may-care indifference to those around him, but who now had another son? Not what we might imagine, especially as she supported him in his desire for freedom from regulation, freedom from school, and encouraged him to let tomorrow look after itself; today was here, now.

One of the other mop tops had to wait until June 1942 to get going, and although his father was absent during his birth – as a volunteer firefighter he was out taking care of fires made by Luftwaffe bombs – unlike John's dad, Jim McCartney wasn't going anywhere. Except in the evenings to earn money playing dance music; he was a pianist, too. The daytime job was as a cotton salesman.

Jim's wife Mary gave birth to their delightful little boy on June the 18th 1942, and she loved the little lad dearly. He had his father's eyes and a mischievous smile; she named him James Paul.

By the time James Paul started his academic life at Stockton Road Primary School, he knew that his charm could get him what he wanted, or, indeed, out of any scrapes he might get into. Not only that, he was also a top pupil. So it was no surprise that he passed his eleven plus examination easily and moved on to the oldest grammar school in Liverpool, the Liverpool Institute. Here, too, now known as Paul to his mates, the young McCartney was head boy in his form. The work came easily to him. Perhaps that's why he would happily sing to himself in bed at night.

Before long, the McCartneys moved into the suburbs, into a council house in Allerton. Life seemed to be running along smooth rails.

And then, Mary discovered that she had breast cancer.

The disease had spread, there was nothing to be done.

At 14, Paul was left without a mother.

Jim McCartney slid marvellously and efficiently into the role of single parent, cooking, cleaning, shopping and looking after his two boys, Paul and Michael. But then came an unexpected new threat to his authority; Lonnie Donegan and his skiffle group.

It was 1956. Drainpipe trousers and floppy hair had taken over the bodies of young British boys like an alien disease – at least, as far as their parents were concerned. They had, inexplicably, morphed into something that was known as a teenager. But what was even worse was the thing that was known as – shudder to think of it – Elvis Presley. And wasn't there another object called Bill Haley?

But it was Lonnie Donegan that Paul McCartney waited around outside the Liverpool Empire Theatre hoping to see. He did see him, and from that point on Paul knew what he wanted; a guitar. Which he got when his father, happy to indulge his son's musical interests, brought one home. Which led Paul to the discovery that it was easier for him to finger pick with his left-hand. Once he had the guitar restrung he was away, rattling through skiffle songs, and when they bored him, he turned to rock 'n' roll. Elvis, of course; also to the Everly Brothers or Little Richard.

Beatle number three had tuned in.

One missing.

In February 1943, the youngest of Harold and Louise Harrison's four children was born, after nine months of being surrounded by exotic music, which his mother listened to on Radio India, and his mother's loud singing. They called the boy George.

George's life in a terraced house with an outdoor toilet and one coal fire for heat, didn't prevent him from being a good student at Dovedale

Primary School, where a certain lad called John Lennon was busy disrupting classes two forms above him.

In 1949, George's life took a decided turn for the better when the family moved into a council house. By the time he passed his eleven plus exam and went to the Liverpool Institute High School for Boys in 1954, music was already high on his list of priorities. Lonnie Donegan, Django Reinhardt and surprisingly, perhaps, George Formby were the men he looked to emulate. Although there was a music class at the Institute, the one instrument George was interested in was not to be found; the guitar. In common with John Lennon, George despised lessons and routines dictated by the classroom. So, despite his excellent memory, he switched off his attention and no punishment could produce even a hint of studiousness in him. His Teddy Boy clothing and his quiff were the outward signs of inward defiance in the face of authority.

But it was Elvis Presley who gave George his Road to Damascus conversion with "Heartbreak Hotel', released in 1956. That same year, his dream came true when his father bought him a Dutch Egmond acoustic guitar. Little did his dad know what chain of events he'd set in motion.

Little did George know, either, of the chain of events that had been set in motion when he chanced to meet another schoolboy from the Liverpool Institute in the bus one day, and a love of popular music cemented their friendship.

His new friend's name was Paul McCartney.

They began to play music together in George's bedroom. Although George didn't have the easy facility of his friend, he more than made up for this with willpower and sheer effort.

Completely taken over by his interest in guitars, before too long, George, his brother Peter and their friend Arthur Kelly had formed

The Rebels, a skiffle group; what else. The last of our nascent superstars was heading into an extraordinary future.

John, by this time, had turned into one of the worst Teddy Boys in Quarry Bank Grammar School, in the opinion of the headmaster. Hardly surprising to learn that John was spending more time with Julia than with Mimi, because his mother had no objection to him wearing drainpipe trousers and drape jackets.

The last line of Mimi's defence collapsed with 'Heartbreak Hotel'. After he had heard it, John could talk about and listen to nothing else. He began to pester Mimi and Julia for a guitar, and it was Mimi who finally cracked. She bought him a steel string model... there would be no hope of 'rescue' for him now. He was a believer, he had found the true path.

The next thing that happened was the formation of The Quarry Men; a skiffle group comprising just John on guitar and his mate Pete on the washboard. Then there were four members when bass and drums were added to a constantly changing lineup. But there was just one person in charge and that was John, standing up front and cracking out skiffle and rock 'n' roll numbers. Enterprising and determined, John lined up gigs in the youth club he still belonged to, and for the school's sixth-form dances.

1957 came around with each of the future Beatles doing his own thing separately from the others. The yearly Woolton fête was held again that summer, and the Quarry Men – with an incensed lead singer who had just had a blazing row with Mimi when she saw him in his full Teddy Boy glory – had been asked to provide some music. For the teenagers in the area this alone was reason to go, and one of those who jumped on his bicycle and headed into Woolton was Paul McCartney.

Paul watched the first performance intensely and was then introduced to the band by a mutual friend of his and John's, the Quarry Men bass player Ivan Vaughan. When the musicians

Circa 1960, lining up outside The Cavern Club

discovered that Paul could not only tune a guitar – they couldn't – and had learned rock 'n' roll songs by heart, miracles that he followed up by showing his prowess on guitar, everyone was impressed. Within a week, John had accepted Paul into the band. It didn't exactly look like a perfect match; Paul was used to getting his own way with charm and a baby face, and John was used to getting his own way with abrupt, if not brutal, directness. But their love for guitars brought them together even though the other members of the group found Paul bossy and slightly arrogant. Paul brought with him changes that initially didn't seem significant but which, in fact, heralded a shift in power and influence. Now, for example, they sported smart stage outfits of white shirts and black trousers. Only Paul and John wore white jackets; no one seemed to spot this obvious statement.

The band continued to gig around the area, John spending as fast as he earned and Paul frugal with his fee. Apollo, god of music, looked down kindly upon his protégés; as the year approached its end, they were booked to appear at a Jazz club in Liverpool town centre. It was underneath some old warehouses.

It was called the Cavern.

ALMOST BUT NOT QUITE

Not that the future looked rosy for our nascent Beatles.

With no exams to help him at the end of his school career, John's future looked nebulous to say the least. But the headmaster of Quarry Bank had recognised the artist in John, and so it was to the Art College in Hope Street that the young Lennon was directed – squeezed in, to be more precise, where, as far as he was concerned, he simply encountered classroom rigidity of a different form. Mimi worried, but kept him fed, clothed and housed in hopes of better times to come.

Paul's turn at exams came the following year, in 1958, and there were plans for him to go into the sixth form. But by now, Paul's focus on school had become blurred and his behaviour had changed; there was competition for his time, especially as skiffle was on its way out and rock 'n' roll records were finding their way towards Liverpool on the Atlantic ships. When Paul began to skip classes, it was clear who was winning the music versus Paul's schoolwork tug-of-war; John Lennon. Once Paul had shown John a song he'd written, another cornerstone in their relationship had been cemented into place, and the two of them began a songwriting relationship that would evolve into one of the most successful in the history of rock 'n' roll, taking them to fame and fortune. They wrote in competition with one another. They always would.

Although Paul's main problem at that moment was how to get rid of the Quarry Men's lead guitarist Eric Griffiths, there was something else playing on Paul's mind around that time; his friend, George, was evolving into a good guitar player and Paul wanted him to join the band. In 1957, George, sporting his new guitar, had a chance to play for the Quarry Men gathered around him. Were they impressed? He was only 14, too young, or so Lennon felt. But George continued to attend their gigs, permitted to sit in if one of the other guitarists failed to turn up. Neither did he allow Lennon's mockery to push him off course.

George's perseverance began to pay off, and he found himself on stage with the band more and more often. Which meant there were too many guitarists. It was obvious that someone had to go; it was Eric Griffiths. Lennon appreciated being able to practice at George's house, where he and George's mother Louise got along very well.

In contrast to John and Mimi.

Mimi was becoming more and more frustrated with John's music, clothes and especially his friends; like the quiet Teddy Boy George Harrison, for some reason. Blazing arguments erupted, and Mimi, afraid of losing John but knowing that she was, seemed unable to make up the lost ground. He would escape the tense atmosphere by going to Julia's house, sometimes for weeks on end, where he was free to do as he pleased.

Until the summer of 1958.

Julia, walking home from Mimi's one night, emerged through

14

a hedge into a main road and was hit by a car. She died instantly.

John's world imploded. He wouldn't admit it, of course. He was seen crying alone. He was constantly drunk. Alcohol and John had already made friends some time before. It would, unfortunately, give free rein to his bitter, often hurtful, sarcasm and his unpredictable temper.

Many girls were put off by John's behaviour. Not so one girl in his school, Cynthia Powell, who, although the butt of his jokes, felt strongly attracted to him. She, too, suffered from poor eyesight, but now dispensed with glasses in public as John did, and changed her neat clothing for more student-like attire. It paid off when John asked her to the dance at the end of term 1958. Against the odds, Lennon and "Cyn" became 'an item'. Cyn also became the object of his violent jealousy.

That year of '58, the Quarry Men, who vanished into Johnny and the Moondogs after entering a talent competition – where they made it through to the final but had to leave before it took place, to catch the last bus home – finally lost their drummer, Colin Hanton, after a drunken performance by his bandmates at a social club. A row on the bus going home led to him taking his drum kit and never coming to another gig. It seemed like the end of the dream. But it wasn't quite.

The story could continue because Pete Best was about to enter the Moondog world; as was Stu Sutcliffe.

Pete Best's mother had opened a coffee club in her house, and through George's introduction, the three guitarists, minus drummer, became a minor hit when they played there. Pete found himself increasingly interested in this rock 'n' roll group. For the moment, though, Pete was to remain an interested onlooker.

Unlike Stu Sutcliffe – the James Dean of Liverpool Art

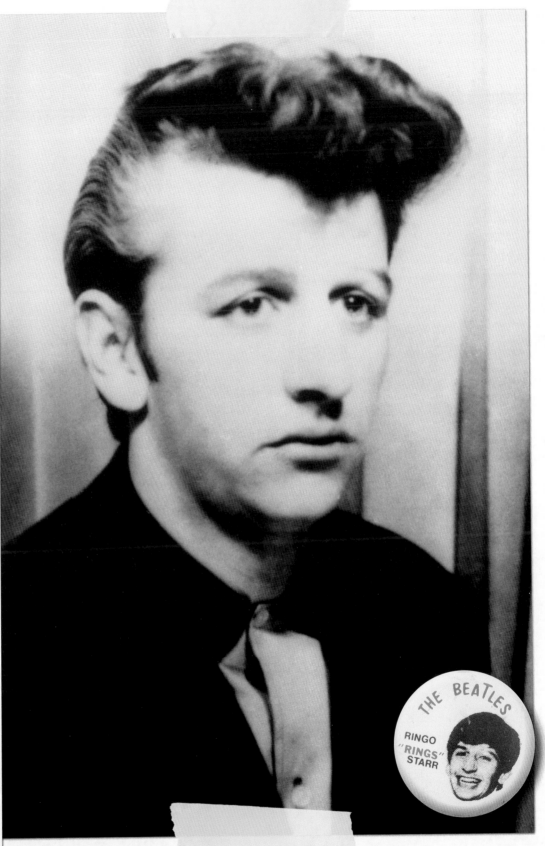

15

1959 while Ringo Starr played drums for 'Rory Storm and the Hurricanes' before joining the Beatles

An early portrait of The Beatles.
L-R: Paul McCartney, Pete Best,
George Harrison & John Lennon

College – who displayed a prodigious creative talent, often helping his fellow student John Lennon, who he met at the student pub Ye Cracke one night. And this bright, talented young man began to enthuse John with his knowledge, which Lennon absorbed in a way he'd never done at school or college.

Stu had developed a personal dress style that owed little to either Teddy Boy or student, and he realised that becoming a musician in the Quarry Men was a way to look even cooler. He became fixated on joining the group, to the extent that he spent the £65 that he'd earned for one of his paintings that had hung in the Walker Art Gallery, on a bass guitar. So Stu got on stage, too, except that he could barely play the enormous bass.

What the group urgently needed, however, to get themselves back on a proper footing, was a drummer, a drummer like the one playing for Liverpool's very own Rory Storm and the

Hurricanes. His name was Richard Starkey, but he preferred to be known as Ringo Starr. The lack of a drummer was proving to be an enormous problem; it lost the boys the chance of some badly needed gigs. Apart from John and Paul writing songs for hours on end, no one seemed capable of remedying the situation.

It was at this point that a man called Allan Williams came to play a vitally important role in the Moondogs' life. Without him, the likelihood of anyone having heard of the Mop Tops today is vanishingly small. Williams owned the Jacaranda coffee bar in Liverpool.

Lennon asked Williams one night if he couldn't do something for the Moondogs; give them a chance to play at the bar, for example. Williams had heard the lads play, and like many others hadn't exactly been bowled over by what he'd heard. Noncommittally, he said that he'd see what he could do – when they got better. What he did do, however, was promise to help find them a drummer, and true to his word, less than one week later, a 36-year-old with his own drum kit had been persuaded to become a Moondog. His name was Tommy Moore. And what's more, he turned out to be a good drummer.

In the meantime, Williams put the band to work - renovating the ladies loos.

Nevertheless, there were opportunities to play when the Royal Caribbean Steel Band, the Jacaranda house band, had a night free.

Then, one day, Liverpool was ablaze with excitement; Billy Fury, one of the towns' own sons, was going to tour the north of England. Even more exciting, Allan Williams had been asked by the entrepreneur Larry Parnes to audition any suitable local musicians as backing groups. Williams decided that Johnny and the Moondogs were ready for the challenge; though not as Johnny and the Moondogs. They needed a new name. Stu scribbled in his sketchbook. The name of Buddy Holly's Crickets, and also the motorcycle gang in the film The Wild One with Marlon Brando popped into his head. He finished writing… The Beetles. It didn't seem ideal, though John turned it into the Beatles, but even that didn't please Allan Williams. In the battle for survival, the name Beatles became the Silver Beatles. So the Silver Beatles would get to audition for Billy Fury and Larry Parnes.

That was the easy part, the competition was fierce; it included Rory Storm (with his drummer Ringo Starr) Cass and the Casanovas and Derry and the Seniors, all experienced bands with first-class equipment.

Afterwards, Allan Williams said that Parnes' only objection to the Silver Beatles was Stu. Parnes couldn't remember Stu but was immediately put off by the drummer, who looked rather ancient surrounded by the young fresh-faced boys.

No contract. So that was that. Except that, once again, it wasn't quite.

A short time afterwards, Parnes organised a two-week Scottish tour with Johnny Gentle, one of his stable of young singers. The Silver Beatles, Parnes said, could back him.

Safe to say, the Silver Beatles went into paroxysms of shock and delight. George, now an apprentice electrician, would have to use his summer holiday entitlement, and Paul persuaded his dad that a two-week break would help his A-level exam revision.

The fact that the Silver Beatles got more applause than Johnny Gentle (who even magnanimously suggested that Parnes should sign them) could be considered as a success story for group. But Tommy Moore ended up in hospital when an inebriated Johnny Gentle crashed the van they were driving in, and by the end of the tour Moore had seen enough of the back streets of Scotland and all of his bandmates, except Stu, but especially John Lennon. Shortly afterwards, he left the group for good.

The tour was a breakthrough of sorts, nonetheless; Williams now added them to his small roster of bands playing in the Liverpool area. They played, minus drummer again, and the Teddy Boy audiences fought amongst themselves. Yet even the musicians weren't immune to the violence of the venues they played in, and Stu was kicked in the head when the Silver Beatles were set upon one night, John breaking his finger in the counter-attack.

Parnes' gigs proved to be a false dawn, and mid-1960 found them strumming in Allan William's strip club.

The real dawn, however, did finally arrive a short time later.

Williams had made a connection to the manager of a place known as the Kaiserkeller Club and had been able to book his band Derry and the Seniors into this club, where they

17

had proved a great success. Such a success, indeed, that he was asked to send another band to the club – which left him with a problem. Rory Storm and Hurricanes would have been the obvious choice, but they had other commitments. Reluctantly, it was the Silver Beatles or nothing.

The Kaiserkeller Club was in Hamburg, northern Germany, and slap bang on the Reeperbahn, at that time the renowned street of iniquity.

John Lennon decided that he was going to Germany come hell or high water; his art career was crumbling into the dust anyway. Stu managed to get a delayed start to his postgrad teacher training course, and Paul had finished his A-levels and got his father's permission without too much of a problem. George at 17 was trusted enough by his family to be let go without opposition.

But – still no drummer.

Fortunate then, that they discovered Pete Best again. And he had a drum kit. Two months in Hamburg, said Paul. Right, said Pete. They were off.

Kitted out with jackets buttoned high at the neck for their stage performances, they set off from Liverpool in a minibus with Allan Williams driving and his wife, brother-in-law and a business associate along for the ride.

It wasn't the Kaiserkeller that awaited them, however, but only a gloomy little cabaret cellar, where for four-and-a-half hours each evening, six at the weekends, they were to give of their best. They would live in three rooms; two alcoves without windows and one large but dirty room. They had to wash in the adjacent cinema toilets.

The severe disappointment was compounded when six bored people, customers and call girls, were their first night audience.

They put on a good show, though, it seems, because word

soon began to spread that there was something worth seeing at the club. And there were compensations after all; free time could be spent on the Reeperbahn watching women mud wrestlers or transvestites. Sexual favours were freely available as was beer – and something slightly more sinister; Preludin, a slimming tablets which boosted metabolism. Only Pete Best stayed aloof from it's seductive hyperactivity inducing characteristics.

With a growing reputation, the Silver Beatles were eventually booked into the Kaiserkeller itself, and when Derry and the Seniors were replaced with Rory Storm and the Hurricanes, the Silver Beatles began to notice the difference in quality between Pete Best's drumming and that of the Hurricanes' drummer Ringo Starr. Also, Best might be the girls' favourite in the club, but they preferred Ringo Starr, who was also funny and friendly.

It was Ringo Starr that they asked to sit in with them and try out some songs in a studio in Hamburg; the last piece of the musical puzzle had slotted in beautifully.

One night, a smartly cool German girl named Astrid Kirchherr was sitting in the Kaiserkeller having been reluctantly taken there by her boyfriend, Klaus Voorman, a passionate aficionado of rock 'n' roll. As soon as her eyes fell on Stu, she knew she was in love. A far cry from the usual type of girl the group met on the Reeperbahn, they had no hesitation in agreeing to let her photograph them. One session turned into many, with industrial Hamburg as a background and meals at Astrid's house as motivation. In return, Astrid and Klaus brought their intellectual friends with them to the Kaiserkeller, and John and Paul could revel in the intelligent conversations.

Astrid's close and very public attention to Stu had its effect on the musician; his clothes changed. So did his experience of intimacy with women. It didn't take long for the other Beatles to change their hairstyles, too. Neither could Astrid avoid noticing tensions within group; John's ruthless sarcasm, the mockery against Stu for his inadequate bass guitar playing, and the jealous dislike of him by Paul, desperate to take over his role in the band.

There was another attraction in Hamburg, one very close to where the boys were in residence at the Kaiserkeller; it was based in a former circus arena called the Hippodrome, and it opened in November 1960 as The Top Ten Club. It was larger and paid bands a lot better than the Kaiserkeller did, and the lads were known to get up on stage there and jam with singers when they were visiting. Despite the boys' contract with the Kaiserkeller, the owner of The Top Ten Club, Peter Eckhorn, persuaded the group to jump ship and join him.

Who knows why... but at that point, the German police looked at George's passport, found that he was only 17 and that it was therefore illegal for him to be in a club after midnight. That was the end of Hamburg for him.

After George's departure, the air seemed to slowly leak out of the Beatles' first German adventure. And when the other lads went to check on their belongings in their former rooms behind the Bambi Kino, and Paul accidentally started some old material smoking with a lit match, the adventure was abruptly halted. A visit by the police ended with Paul and Pete Best being deported. John and Stu followed them and the Silver Beatles arrived back in England rich in life experience and better musicians but wondering what the future might now hold for a bunch of out of work rock and rollers.

Poster for one of The Beatles Hamburg shows supporting Rory Storm & The Hurricanes, then containing Ringo Starr

AUF WIEDERSEHEN HAMBURG

It snowed in Liverpool that winter. The Silver Beatles' career prospects had gone cold, too. But Lady Luck hadn't abandoned them; she was prepared to have one more attempt at hoisting them up by their guitar straps.

Brian Kelly organised dances at town halls and other venues in Liverpool, and on the 27th of December 1960 he arrived at Litherland Town Hall for one concert that he had arranged with a group known as the Silver Beatles.

Whatever might have happened to their musicianship skills in Hamburg was of secondary importance; by the time the concert was over, girls were swarming around them asking for their autographs. The principal centre of their attention was, as usual, drummer Pete Best. Brian Kelly recognised potential profit when he saw it, and the band was booked for more appearances at other venues.

It was Pete's mum Mona, acting as unofficial agent, who first put the idea of staging a rock 'n' roll group at the Cavern Club to its owner Ray McFall. In January 1961, he allowed them onto his stage. He soon knew that he had not made a mistake; on the few afternoons during the week when the Silver Beatles played at the Cavern Club for two 45-minute spots there would be a queue of young girls waiting to get in. The effect that the band's modest fame had on the musicians' parents was varied; Paul's dad accepted it, Mimi was incensed, and George's mum yelled enthusiastically with the rest of the girls.

Now it was Gerry and the Pacemakers' turn to come back from Hamburg with tales of life gleefully misspent on the Reeperbahn. Their interest rekindled, the Silver Beatles arranged to play at the Top Ten Club again in April of 1961.

They arrived in Hamburg to be welcomed by Astrid, whose emotional support Stu badly needed as he had learned shortly before that he would not be admitted to Liverpool Art College for his teacher training diploma. The boys returned to their former life of alcohol, willing barmaids, and 'Prellys', the slimming pills.

It was now that the animosity between Stu and Paul reached its zenith, when Stu attacked Paul, who had said something about Astrid that Stu took exception to. Stu was smaller than Paul, who then began to beat him up.

Astrid and her friends persuaded Stu to apply for art college in Hamburg, and the quality of his work was so good that he was not only admitted but was also given a maintenance grant. Slowly, his life as a Beatle faded, and his life as a student artist, filled with nights of almost maniacal work, took over as though he was already afraid of what the future might hold. Headaches, which had bothered him for many years, became more intense making him even more bad tempered toward Astrid. Stu decided to stay and study in Hamburg and marry Astrid.

For one boy, this turn of events made his heart bound with joy, for his greatest wish had now come true; Paul was now

21

Standing outside Paul's home (left to right) George Harrison, John Lennon, Paul McCartney

22

Astrid Kirchherr and Stuart Sutcliffe in Hamburg, Germany in April 1961

the bass player in the Silver Beatles.

At this point, the boys decided to tell Allan Williams that because they had secured the engagement themselves, he would not be receiving his 10% commission.

Understandably hurt by this underhand treatment, he wrote a long letter expressing his upset, but he didn't pursue his threats to have them blacklisted. Sadly, so ended the relationship with the most important man in the Beatles' lives up until that time.

Back in Liverpool, gigs in the sauna-like atmosphere of the Cavern continued, though it was beginning to seem, to John at least, like a dead-end, and he wrote often to Stu, who seemed to have chosen a more adventurous life in a foreign country.

Not far away, another young man was feeling equally listless, running a successful music shop that his father had bought called NEMS. He was a conscientious employer to the other members of his staff, but a perfectionist, and it was not unknown for him to fly into a temper when some trivial inconsistency came to his attention. The young man also had a secret that very few people at the start of the 1960s would have been brave enough to have made public; he was gay.

Brian Epstein was 27 years old when a customer in NEMS first mentioned a Liverpool group known as the Beatles to him. He hadn't heard of them but promised the customer he would investigate further. But finding information from wholesalers proved difficult. Undaunted, Epstein discovered that the group played in a club just a stone's throw from the shop. He decided to visit. Fortunately for popular music and four Liverpool rock 'n' roll musicians, he didn't turn around and walk home when the dank smell and heat rose up to his nostrils as he descended the stairs to the Cavern Club.

Against his own expectations, Epstein stayed to watch two of the Beatles' sets. And not simply because of the leather-clad musicians enjoying themselves with their banter and guitars on stage. By now, something of a Beatles sound was emerging from the boys' throats, and Epstein found a novel idea floating

23

Arnhem War Memorial, Netherlands, during a journey to Hamburg, 1960. (L-R) Beatles manager Allan Williams and wife Beryl, Lord Woodbine, Stuart Sutcliffe, Paul McCartney, George Harrison and Pete Best

around in his head. Brian went to see them again on several other occasions as the idea began to solidify; he wanted to become the Beatles' manager.

Brian had been busy; he had formed NEMS Enterprises and gave the lads contracts, and because of his contacts through the store had been able to arrange for the Silver Beatles to audition for the Decca record company in London. Despite being assured by Mike Smith of Decca that the audition had gone well, the boys weren't happy with their performance. They lost out, anyway, and Decca signed Brian Poole and the Tremoloes, who were based closer to their offices in the south of London.

It took two attempts with the group before John Lennon could be

persuaded to squeeze out a yes to let Brian become their manager. And although John didn't know it, he was the real reason for Brian's interest, the one that Brian really wanted to help. As he said to Mimi to assuage her fears, "the others don't matter...". For that devotion, Brian was going to suffer beneath cutting sarcasm from John that would often reduce him to tears.

Undaunted, Brian took up the cudgels again on the Beatles' behalf and set to work talking to the other record companies. There was little interest in a group sounding similar to the Shadows when solo singers were now the latest musical fashion. All in all, it was a very dispiriting start. Brian did all he could to get the lads' careers onto an upwards spiral, bluffing, if necessary, and giving them pep talks, restyling them, against John's initial opposition, of course; but his middle-class tones and attitudes made little headway with the rough northern promoters. The best he could come up with was another engagement in Hamburg.

As 1961 passed into 1962, there was sad news to add to the despondency. Stu Sutcliffe was still in Hamburg with Astrid, but his headaches had been increasing in intensity. Still attending art school, he collapsed one day in February. By March he was suffering periods of temporary blindness with the pain becoming unbearable. That month the attacks became so bad that he and Astrid were taken to hospital in an ambulance. He died in her arms.

It was the day the Beatles arrived in Hamburg for a six-week engagement. They had a concert to play that night. George and

Pete Best couldn't stop the tears from flowing, and Paul was devastated and filled with guilt for the past animosity he had shown to Stu. John put on an outward show of indifference, but his attitude and words gave strength to Astrid. Later, Stu's sister revealed that John had apparently assaulted Stu, kicking him in the head – and that the boy's relationship may have been more than purely platonic – which left John with deep guilt that he may have caused Stu's death. Only after Lennon's death would his violence towards others, women and men, become common knowledge.

This time around, the band was in the far more opulent surroundings of the Star Club. But the Preludin was, if anything, used even more liberally, especially by John, whose outrageous

25

Hamburg, Germany during their residency at The Star Club in May 1962

behaviour on and off stage was fuelled by pills and alcohol to the extent that he would sometimes be "foaming at the mouth".

Back in London, Brian was not quite at that foaming at the mouth stage, although he might have felt that the day was not far off as he walked into a recording studio to have the Beatles' demo tapes converted to an acetate. If he were going to foam at the mouth, it was soon to be for a different reason. The engineer liked the sound and played the audition to Syd Coleman in the publishing company above the studio. Coleman also liked what he heard, and so

the audition ended up in the hands of George Martin of Parlophone, a subsidiary of EMI. Faintly, the sound of a door opening might have been audible.

Martin was not overly enthusiastic but thought that there might be a nugget of talent worth pursuing. And he needed new product. If it didn't require too much work, this band might just fit the bill. He would give The Beatles a studio audition in June.

Abbey Road Studios.
1962.
The 6th of June.
A Wednesday.

No one would have laid a bet that George Martin and a group of scruffy Liverpudlian musicians would end up enjoying each other's company. But that's what happened. A mutual admiration of Spike Milligan helped.

The audition itself then started, but with the Beatles churning out some corny songs and only "Love Love Me Do" bearing any resemblance to something Martin might use, it was inconclusive. Still, Martin was not dismissive, and he did take Brian to one side and utter the words "if we make a record". He also said that in that case, he didn't want to have Pete Best as the drummer.

Without knowing what Martin had said, both Paul and George wanted to be rid of Best anyway. Brian kept the news to himself trying to work out what to do. Nothing happened whilst the band carried out more engagements following the audition.

Martin's lack of enthusiasm just about brought an offer in July. Four titles to be recorded within the year, one penny royalty for each double-sided record.

26

George Martin 1960

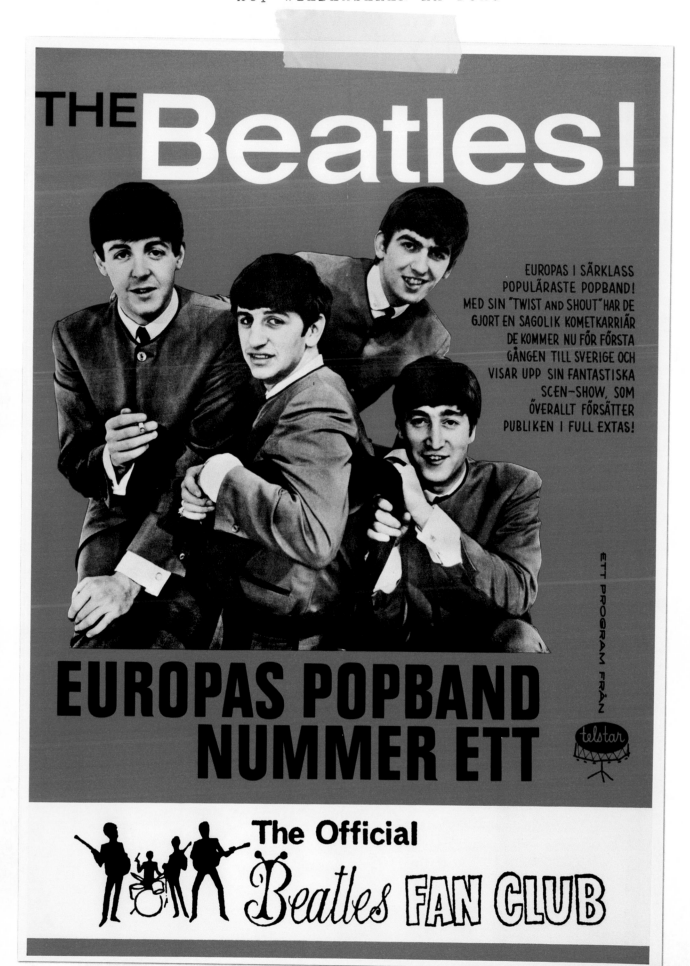

27

No matter; it was an offer that any band would be delighted with.

August turned out to be a month that would bring emotional turmoil into the lives of two of the band members; John discovered that his girlfriend Cynthia was pregnant and decided that they would have to get married. Mimi couldn't bear to be present, but Paul and George were – as was Brian, acting as John's best man. A chicken lunch followed.

On the 16th, Brian broke the news to Pete Best that the boys wanted him out of the group. Pete had been within a whisker of massive stardom. Instead, someone else would now taste the golden fruits of fame.

The drummer that George went looking for in Liverpool had spent time in Hamburg, too, got homesick for Liverpool, had returned to Rory Storm and Hurricanes and was now in Skegness for the summer.

John finally phoned him to offer him £25 pounds a week to swap bands. Ringo Starr agreed. The last of the Beatles had found his way home.

On September the 11th, the new lineup arrived at Abbey Road Studios for the recording session. Against his initial reservations, Martin decided to use 'Love Me Do' and 'PS I Love You', two Lennon-McCartney songs, spiced up with harmonica, maracas and tambourine. The session went without a hitch.

There was more excitement in October; Brian had needed to redraft the contracts with the lads, because Paul and George were underage, and get them witnessed by the parents. On the 4th, their single was released, 10,000 copies of which Brian had bought, 10,000 being the magic number, apparently, for a top 20 hit. Decca showed no interest in promoting it, but it worked its way up to number 17 in the NME by December the 13th. The world did not explode with joy.

Also in October, Brian had arranged for Little Richard to play at the New Brighton Tower, one of several concerts with big names he had set up with The Beatles second on the bill. Brian was now finding his feet as a manager to the extent that he was able to get Little Richard back again, to the Liverpool Empire Theatre this time, always conscious that the reflected light from the stars of the day would shine on his own group.

Life was now revving up, for his band found themselves back in Abbey Road Studios on the 26th of November. They came with a new song, which Martin had already heard, but which they had reworked. By the end of the recording session, thoroughly enjoyed by everyone, apparently, George Martin was enthusiastic enough to say to the boys that they had just made "your first number one". The song was called 'Please Please Me'.

Now it was time for their potential new publisher, Dick James, to spring into action. In the presence of a dubious Brian, he picked up the phone and five minutes later had secured the Beatles a slot on a Saturday night television show called Thank Your Lucky Stars. It was clear who was going to be publishing the Beatles music from then on.

The most exciting and successful year the four had ever had was to finish with another stint in Hamburg and two weeks at the Star Club; this time for 1000 Deutschmarks. By pure chance, the recording exists of one of their performances in Germany. In the noise of the huge hall, the obviously drunk singers mess up words and musical phrases, yell at the audience in mangled Deutsch-Scouse and whack out their old musical chestnuts.

There's one interesting side note to the recording; on the tape, another group can be heard playing at the Star Club; Kingsize Taylor and the Dominoes, singing 'Twist and Shout' by Bert Burns and Phil Medley.

29

The Beatles, completed 1962

IS SOMEONE SCREAMING?

When the Beatles appeared on Thank Your Lucky Stars in January 1963 in the middle of the worst winter for almost one hundred years, they resembled mime artists more than rock musicians. This was thanks to a sound that would follow them around for a very long time – and make them very wealthy; the sound of screaming teenage girls.

The girls' new idols looked very different from the usual crop of pop singers; their suit jackets were buttoned up to the neck and their hairstyles resembled neat round bushes as the boys bobbed about in front of the microphones apparently singing. The magnetic effect was instantaneous not only amongst the studio audience but also amongst the music press, where the new single 'Please Please Me' had begun to rise into the UK top 10 and words such as "vigour and vitality" could be heard. The BBC compère of Thank Your Lucky Stars called them "the most accomplished group to emerge since the Shadows". It was obvious to George Martin and many others that he had struck gold.

He didn't have to wait long for the proof; the lads were out on tour with Helen Shapiro, and by all accounts, the young 16-year-old Helen enjoyed travelling with the leather-clad boys, who were always fun, always witty, always active. On the 2nd of March, anyone connected with the Liverpool lads could hardly believe their eyes. 'Please Please Me' was number one in Melody Maker's top 20. It was soon obvious to everyone that the intensity of the Beatles' applause each night meant that the group would soon be in a league of their own; for the remainder of the tour, they had a higher billing.

Brian must have been unbearably excited, although outwardly he showed it to no one as he fielded an endless stream of phone calls in his office. It was his voice that betrayed him.

George Martin was an old hand in the music business and he knew that this success had to be carefully nurtured or it would shrivel and die in no time as many other one-hit wonders had. There had to be a follow-up LP, and the idea he came up with was to record fourteen songs that the Beatles played at the Cavern Club, songs such as 'Do You Want to Know a Secret', 'I Saw Her Standing There' and 'Twist and Shout'. It was a long recording session; thirteen hours, and just twenty days after the single had reached number one, their first album, 'Please Please Me' was released with the four lads in burgundy suits smiling down from a balcony on the cover. The music press were impressed that most of the songs had been written by the

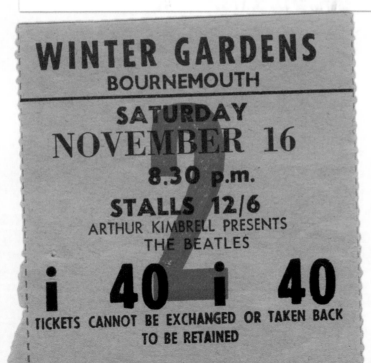

WINTER GARDENS
BOURNEMOUTH

SATURDAY
NOVEMBER 16
8.30 p.m.

STALLS 12/6
ARTHUR KIMBRELL PRESENTS
THE BEATLES

2

i 40 i 40

TICKETS CANNOT BE EXCHANGED OR TAKEN BACK
TO BE RETAINED

31

The Beatles with their manager Brian Epstein

Backstage portraits

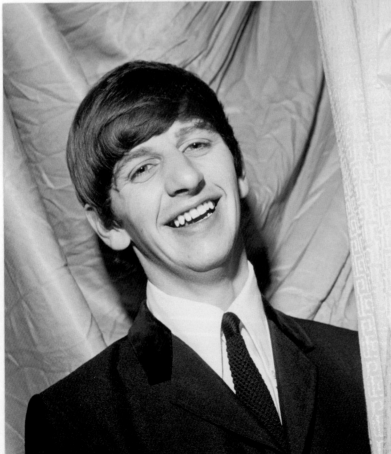

lads themselves; unusual in the pop world of the time.

Brian began to learn that he could ask for a larger fee for The Beatles to appear and promoters were willing to pay it. And he knew that NEMS enterprises and its protégés The Beatles were going to need legal eagles in London to shield them from the sharks in the business. He chose M. A. Jacobs, who had dealt with such luminaries as Marlene Dietrich. Jewish, like Brian, David Jacobs and the manager would form a ring of iron around The Beatles that only death could break.

For John Lennon, balanced on the edge of superstardom, perhaps a baby was not on his list of wants; but a baby he got that he had helped to make, with Cynthia. He called the boy Julian in honour of his mother Julia. And then told Cynthia that he was going on holiday to Spain – with Brian. This was Brian's attempt to make another dream come true, which John would have known when he accepted Brian's offer – and which did involve 'male bonding', as John admitted later.

Sensing that he was on the edge of something exciting, Brian dared to sign another boy group from Liverpool, Gerry and the Pacemakers. Their first single, 'How Do You Do It?', also went straight to number one, and for the first time the music press began to latch onto the fact that there was such a thing as a consistent Liverpool or Mersey sound. So Brian took on yet another Liverpool lad, Billy J Kramer, backed by the Dakotas from Manchester, and he hit the jackpot yet again when Kramer's single' Do You Want to Know a Secret?' written by Lennon and McCartney, went up to number 2 by mid-May. Liverpool was becoming the go-to-place for entertainment, and the once maligned accent was now an open sesame for many pop groups, or even entertainers, like Ken Dodd, Cilla Black and Jimmy Tarbuck.

Further success with Brian's first group wasn't long in coming, either; even though the music reviewers were less than enthusiastic about the new song, the fans were not, and by April the 27th, 'From Me to You', which John and Paul had written in the bus during the Helen Shapiro tour, was number one. Gerry and the Pacemakers weren't far behind at number 3. The great Liverpool wave had begun and Brian was beginning to feel that his Midas touch might lead him to a musical empire as head of NEMS Enterprises, which now had offices in London. He looked around for more talent, and by the middle of the year had signed a group known as the Fourmost as well as a ballad singer, Tommy Quigley. Had he not, he might have felt able to sign another group that he was offered; but he decided to call a halt for the time being. Thus he passed up the chance to sign the Rolling Stones. When the Beatles met the Stones one night, they were impressed with the musicianship and the choice of clothing and remained friendly rivals from then on.

The hits kept coming, too; Gerry Marsden and Billy J. Kramer both reached number one again, Kramer with a McCartney and Lennon song, 'Bad to Me'. Brian could boast that he had three groups at numbers one, two and three in the charts, an achievement unequalled by any other impresario since. Perhaps chastened by his experience with the Stones, Brian had now taken on a young female singer from Liverpool, Cilla Black, and George Martin recorded her singing, what else, a Lennon and McCartney song; 'Love of the Loved'. Either singing or songwriting, the lads were beginning to dominate the British charts.

Everyone connected with the musicians in the band was made to feel that their lives were changing, whether it was John's absence from Cynthia and the baby living on the lower floor of Mimi's house, the girls swarming around George Harrison's parents' house, or the money that suddenly began to appear in large quantities in Ringo's room. The deluge of adoring fans meant that Paul had to celebrate his 21st birthday that year at his aunt's house in Birkenhead.

For Paul, an even larger change was about to take place,

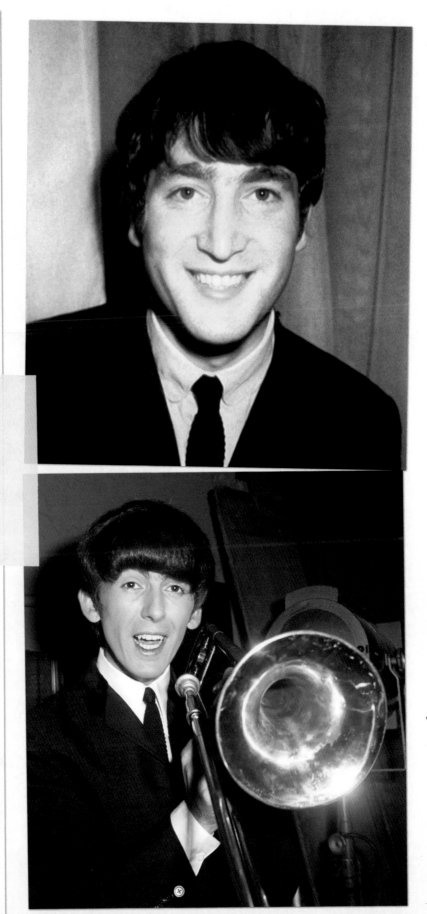

Backstage portraits

34

Wearing policeman's helmets, George, Paul, John and Ringo salute the press as they are escorted from the back of a black Austin police van at the stage door before a performance at the Hippodrome Theatre because on April the 18th, following a concert at the Royal Albert Hall in London, where the Beatles were the headline act, he met the actress Jane Asher. Although all the Beatles had big eyes for the young girl, Asher was just 17; they realised that sweet-faced Paul McCartney was going to be the anointed one. This well-heeled, genteel girl, whose father, a well-known psychiatrist, was a senior physician at Central Middlesex Hospital, lived in a world of which Paul had often dreamed, enviously. After that night, they would frequently be spotted in the West End of London or at smart parties.

Ringo, too, was romantically involved with a girl he had met at the Cavern Club. Mary Maureen Cox, 'Mo' to her friends, and they were soon seen out and about together.

Before the end of the year, Brian would move his organisation to London lock stock and barrel, would find a new flat and begin to entertain in a style befitting an impresario, befriending show business celebrities. As his empire grew, and the Beatles' lives became more complex, so he came to rely on his lawyer David Jacobs and his accountants Bryce, Hammer and Isherwood more and more. His accountant, a man from Czechoslovakia with the somewhat James Bond villain name of Dr. Strack, made The Beatles into a limited company, which prudently hoarded much of their earnings awaiting the evil taxman. And although promoters, record companies and cinema owners earned handsomely from them, the group were still operating on contracts agreed sometime before. Unfortunately, Brian was not yet a sharp Londoner, and before long the sharp Londoners knew that Brian was not street wise. At the beginning, therefore, the boys had very little ready cash. Nonetheless, Brian strove to be honest and fair in his dealings with The Beatles at all times, going so far as to voluntarily give them 10% of his own company, NEMS

Enterprises, in compensation for his 25% fee as their manager; an extraordinary gesture in a cut-throat and selfish industry.

As their lives began to speed up, with a bestselling single and album helping to bear them aloft, The Beatles returned to Abbey Road and recorded 'She Loves You'. In its way it was melodically innovative, using chords not often found in pop music at the time, and its theme of a boy, not a girl, being told in the narrative that his girlfriend loves him, was also a reversal of roles. 'She Loves You' stayed at number one for almost two months. The mainstream media was now beginning to sit up and take notice of this pop group that had topped the poll to find the year's most popular recording artists, in the Melody Maker in autumn 1963.

The snowball effect was evident, too, when the band undertook a short concert tour to Sweden; five dates at the end of October, where their reception by the Swedish girls was no less frantic than it had been in England. When Heathrow airport was filled with hundreds of screaming fans upon their return, it was obvious that something extraordinary was happening to the four young Liverpudlians.

Another sign that they were on their way to the stars was their headline appearance on the top variety program in Britain, Sunday Night at the London Palladium. The media whipped the event up into what would later be termed Beatlemania, turning the few girls waiting outside into thousands; fake news even then; but no matter, it all helped to sell papers. Before long, it would be tens of thousands, each Beatles' concert producing audiences of weeping teenage girls screaming themselves into hysteria, a phenomenon no self-respecting Fleet Street newspaper could ignore for long. Venues were besieged for tickets, bruises were becoming part and parcel of the fray.

The media were only too happy to put out the image of four cute, mop-haired musicians who also happened to

35

be intelligent and funny. Their songs showed that they were still tough Liverpudlians, but their characters were marbled with sensitivity and they were cleverly observant of their fellow humans.

Who would print the reality? It certainly wouldn't be written by their official fan magazine editor Peter Jones. No one wanted to disturb the cosy image. So for the moment, no one would know that the boys already loathed the nightly performances so much that they would have to be forced onto the stage, George, in particular, revolted by the deafening screaming and the flying toys and sweets. No one would know of the steady stream of young girls led to the lads in any quiet place that could be found; know of their ugly mockery of others that would sometimes turn into physical violence. Nor would there be any mention of the loud arguments that often broke out between them, and the occasions when Brian would be involved in rows, too. If anything had come through about The Beatles' private lives, they would certainly not have been invited to the Royal Command Variety Performance in London that November to perform alongside Marlene Dietrich and Harry Secombe, amongst others, for Princess Margaret and the Queen Mother.

Thousands of screaming girls gathered outside and inside the theatre in Leicester Square. By the time the Beatles had finished their four songs, they had won over their royal audience and all the other bejewelled spectators as well. The Beatles, it seemed, had conquered the entire country. As the Daily Mirror enthused: "You have to be a real sour square not to love the... happy, handsome Beatles". In 1960s Britain, a country still suffering from lingering postwar gloom, the papers knew what they needed to do to sell copy. So Fleet Street began to analyse every aspect of Beatlemania; its vocabulary, its sexual potency, its apparently clean, youthfully uninhibited fun.

The Beatles' record company, EMI, aware of the rapidly expanding financial possibilities surrounding the group, hurried out their second album, With the Beatles, after advance orders of 250,000 copies. It was followed by 'I Want to Hold Your Hand', their fifth single, which generated advanced orders of over one million copies; an immediate number one hit.

London now became the centre of gravity for all four Beatles. Ringo and George took the opportunity to move in together in the same block as Brian, whereas John and Cynthia found a flat in Kensington. They were all soon smoked out by the fans, and then there were adoring girls dripping all over the 'secret' premises.

As for Paul, no one quite knew where he was except that Jane Asher was with him. In fact, he now spent all of his time with the Asher family.

The g-force that the Beatles were generating could now no longer be ignored in America, where previously even George Martin had been unable to pierce anti-British attitudes by Americans used to calling the tune. The Beatles were about to sweep that prejudice clean out of the window.

36

CIVIC RECEPTION FOR

"THE BEATLES"

FRIDAY, 10TH JULY, 1964

FROM 7·0 P.M. TO 8·0 P.M.

No 149

ADMIT ONE PERSON

37

Palladium Theatre during rehearsals for their appearance on ATV's 'Val Parnell's Sunday Night At The London Palladium show

George Martin had managed, with great difficulty, to persuade American record industry executives to take the Beatles' hits, but when they reluctantly did so, the singles failed to make a dent in anything except George's confidence. Nonetheless, Brian made another attempt and managed to get Capitol records to release 'I Want to Hold Your Hand', also without much enthusiasm. Unlike talk show host Ed Sullivan who, with his sometimes reluctant ear to the ground, arranged for The Beatles to appear on his show on the 9th and 16th of February 1964, unaware of the British tornado he was about to unleash on the American people.

The trip didn't appear to have been a great success for Brian. But at least, he consoled himself, he had managed to get Billy J. Kramer signed with Liberty Records.

America seemed a long way away during The Beatles' freezing, six-week tour of one-night concerts in winter 1963/64. The workload had increased dramatically, because at the same time as they were performing, they were writing songs for a film to be made in the spring and preparing for a Christmas special. And despite the screaming crowds, they were still spending the nights in second-rate hotels.

At least they had created a log jam in the British charts that Christmas; 'I Want to Hold Your Hand' was at number one, and there were six other Beatles' songs in the top 20. Their other singles were already selling in the millions.

But even if Brian had not quite grasped the fact, to use military parlance, the balloon had gone up. There was a growing realisation that the teenage market was huge and it would buy not just records but anything else that bore their idols' image. Unfortunately, Brian's incomprehension of the scale of what merchandising could achieve led to confusion and more lost financial opportunities for the Liverpool lads giving their all on stage.

Not that merchandising in Europe was much of a problem after the concert in Paris on January the 15th 1964, where the audience seemed bored and the reviews next day were lukewarm to dismissive. For the moment, the French had proved to be resistant to Beatlemania.

Still, something more dramatic had happened across the Atlantic; 'I Want to Hold Your Hand' had hit number one in the American top one hundred.

No sooner had The Beatles begun to seep into the psyche of American youngsters than they inevitably began to seep into the psyche of American music executives. The radio plays of 'I Want to Hold Your Hand' started an avalanche of enquiries on the streets that no American A&R man worth his salt could afford to ignore. Suddenly, Capitol released the With The Beatles LP, which they had renamed Meet the Beatles, and it, too, shot to the top of the album charts. Caught on the hop, Capitol had to swiftly arrange publicity for the band's forthcoming TV appearance for which the Ed Sullivan Show had been inundated with 50,000 applications for seats, greater interest than even Elvis had received.

Pan Am flight 101 bearing its four mop-tops took off from Heathrow amidst pandemonium amongst the one thousand fans and the words of Alan Livingston, President of Capitol in the boy's ears: "We don't think the Beatles will do anything in this market".

The music industry could just about be forgiven for not hearing the sound of a phenomenon taking off as well.

The British invasion had begun.

39

Beatles perform on stage, 1964

STAMPING

OUT DETROIT

There weren't one thousand fans waiting for them in America, though; there were five thousand. Not even the Beatles themselves could believe their eyes. Yelling girls were everywhere, some of them being chased away by police, their combined decibel level making the questions of 200 journalists and photographers almost inaudible. The lads flicked away the questions they could hear with Liverpudlian audacity, which seemed to endear them to everyone. When asked about the campaign in Detroit to stamp out the Beatles, Paul replied that they had their own campaign to stamp out Detroit. And he got away with it.

It was the lads' first taste of how dangerous fame could become, and they were manhandled into their limousine by police, who left their finger marks on the boys for a long time after.

The Plaza Hotel on Fifth Avenue had given The Beatles ten interconnecting suites, where they gave interviews and were besieged by teenage fans desperately attempting entry in any way possible. When they set off next morning for the TV studio, there was a sea of girls and police around the limousine, and 73 million Americans were waiting to see them jiggle about in grainy black-and-white.

"We came out of nowhere with funny hair, looking like marionettes or something", recalled Paul McCartney.

Whilst fathers saw them as a threat, mothers and children rejoiced. A new era had begun, and America, reeling from

President Kennedy's assassination not long before, was ready and willing to be mesmerised.

This show smashed television viewing records in the US and the press were not adverse to their charms, though the faint praise could not conceal their bafflement; "Asexual and homely" and "A fine mass placebo", they murmured.

Next morning, The Beatles faced press for hour upon hour of inane questions, which they fielded with amazing good humour and patience, obviously enjoying their newfound fame. Brian, on the other hand, maintaining an aloof stance away from the melee, seemed to be drowning in some psychological drama of his own. At the time, he would often been seen crying alone, and he would be seen crying alone again in the future. Perhaps it was fear that made it impossible for him to enjoy to the full this extraordinary life he had done so much to create; fear that he had helped to give birth to a monster he could not contain. Perhaps he wished that he was one of the monsters.

He was certainly unprepared for the ruthlessness of American business methods as anyone and everyone cashed in on The Beatles, with Brian having no idea who was doing what where or when. He had, though, finally understood what catastrophic deals he had allowed to be struck for the merchandising, which was being sold in unheard of quantities and would reap $5 million worth of business by the end of the year, of which he and The Beatles would receive but a fraction; 10%. The man receiving the 90%, Nicky Byrne, now had a private helicopter and chauffeur-

41

driven limousines. Byrne happily realised that
Brian truly did not have a grip on the situation at
all.

The Beatles were soon due to give their first
American concert in Washington, where they arrived
by train, thanks to the snow in New York, because
they refused to fly in a blizzard. They were met by
3000 teenagers at the station and 7000 at the venue,
where they were pelted with America's harder version
of the jelly baby, the jellybean, the result of a joke
George Harrison made about liking jelly babies.

But amongst the continuing jibes about their
haircuts, the lads were now infiltrating the
establishment, having been invited to the British
Embassy, where they were subjected to less than
cordial treatment, which they rose above admirably.
And as their star ascended, they had their photos
taken with a brash young boxer known as Cassius

— THE BEATLES —
CITY PARK STADIUM
NEW ORLEANS, LA.
WEDNESDAY EVENING 8:00 P. M.
SEPT'BR
16
1964
ADMIT ONE
EST. PR.   4.32
FED. TAX   .33
WEL. TAX   .22
C & S TAX   .13
TOTAL
$5.00
NO REFUNDS FOR ANY REASON
EXCEPT CANCELLATION OF SHOW.

23434   23434

GOOD ONLY
WEDNESDAY EVE.
SEPTEMBER
16
1964
GLOBE TICKET CO., INC., ATLANTA

THE BEATLES
CITY PARK STADIUM — NEW ORLEANS, LA.

HOLLYWOOD BOWL
2301 N. Highland Ave.
HOLLYWOOD   CALIFORNIA
AUG.
23
1964
THE BEATLES
SAT. EVE. AUG. 23, 8:00 P.M.
PRICE $4.00
NO REFUNDS — NO EXCHANGES

RESERVED
J 17 38
$4.00

42

The Beatles arrive at Kennedy Airport for the first time
for a 10 day tour, 1964 in New York City

43

Portrait in front of an American
Flag, New York City, 1964

44

Clay. It would not be long before everyone was clamouring for their favours.

None of the hysteria abated for their two New York concerts at Carnegie Hall, or as they flew into Miami for the second appearance on the Ed Sullivan Show. They left the airport and 7000 hyped-up fans, who smashed glass doors and windows despite the police presence, before entering another besieged hotel. They then proceeded to smash more television records; 75 million Americans were said to have watched the Ed Sullivan Show and The Beatles' second appearance. They would appear for a third time in a pre-recorded sequence introduced by Sullivan with the following words:

"All of us on the show are so darned sorry, and sincerely sorry, that this is the third and thus our last current show with The Beatles, because these youngsters from Liverpool, England, and their conduct over here, not only as fine professional singers but as a group of fine youngsters, will leave an imprint on everyone over here who's met them."

A friendly cop arranged for the four to be smuggled out of the Deauville Hotel in Miami in the back of butcher's truck.

Extraordinary times for four Liverpool lads.

But then, they were extraordinary lads, as the Rolling Stones' manager Andrew Oldham could confirm when a chance meeting with John and Paul led to them simply giving the Stones a song they were writing; "I Wanna Be Your Man". The Rolling Stones never looked back.

The Beatles could afford to be generous, as their songs were being gobbled up by a record buying public eager for new tunes, and their latest offering, 'Can't Buy Me Love' had reached number one in Britain and America at the same time, the first record ever to do so, with advance sales of over 3 million.

Portraits from 1964

That year of 1964 saw the Beatles with the world in the palms of their hands. They made their first feature film, which was eventually called A Hard Day's Night – a phrase coined by Ringo – filming a kind of permanent chase scene in ten minutes bursts, because that was as long as they could ever get before being inundated by crowds.

They crept further up the ladder of acceptability when Princess Margaret attended the premiere and had drinks with them afterwards enjoying herself enormously.

In America, the film earned $1.3 million in its first week, complete with screaming audiences.

The roundabout began to turn even faster as they toured the world, always to the same screaming reception inside and out, even when Ringo was replaced temporarily by Jimmy Nicholl because he was having his tonsils taken out. Maureen quickly went to visit him. Ringo proposed to her in the hospital, and she said yes.

45

THE BEATLES
in THEIR FIRST FULL LENGTH HILARIOUS, ACTION-PAC
6 EXCITING NEW SONGS!

A HARD DAY'S NIC

also starring WILFRID BRAMBELL

produced by WALTER SHENSON   original screenplay by ALUN OWEN   directed b

47

The Beatles run from the police in a still from 'A Hard Day's Night'

Whether it was Scandinavia, Australia – with the largest crowd ever, 300,000 people – or the Far East, the group never saw much more than the inside of a hotel room, a dressing room, limousine or an aeroplane, unable to distinguish one country from another, often not even knowing which country they were in.

They had time to realise that they were back in America in August, though, because they had 23 cities to visit, 23 sets of mayors, senators and their wives and rows of worthies, plus the best call girls money could buy – and if they ever doubted that they were in America, the sale of their hotel bed linen and the never-ending visits by handicapped children whose parents hoped for some Jesus-like miracle from four Liverpudlian musicians, would always be a reminder. A reminder, too, of how maniacal their world had

become, how surrounded by chaos they were; girls falling onto the stage, girls having to be rescued from impossible places, fans charging planes, armies of flashing camera bulbs, hail storms of jelly babies, police storming fans in vast auditoria and always, always the interminable sound of screaming.

And what of the boys themselves amongst all of this furore? What did they do when they weren't on stage, or once they had used up the shrunken amount of free time they had, to buy anything they could lay their hands from suits and shirts to clothes, cameras, watches and houses in the stockbroker belt south of London? There was money aplenty now for the Jaguars and Aston Martins, the Rolls-Royces and Ferrari's. The money also bought drugs in any quantities they wished, which helped to liven up the days and nights now that daily champagne, sex, money and stardom to excess had proven to be things you could get bored with. Marijuana had been introduced into their lives that year, too, with the result that for the entire length of filming for their second film, Help!, they were all happily high. George and John also had their first experience of LSD that year when they unknowingly swallowed it in coffee at their dentist's house. The resulting paranoia terrified them. Initially. Subsequently, Lennon and Harrison used the drug regularly.

George was dating a 19-year-old model call Pattie Boyd, one of the icons of fashionable England in the early 60s, who soon discovered that with The Beatles not much was private about their private life and that she, too, would be forced to leave hotels in disguise.

Ringo was still with Maureen Cox, his girlfriend from the Cavern Club era. In January 1965, 18-year-old Maureen had found out that she was pregnant. So, with Brian as best man, Ringo and Maureen were married on the 11th of February 1965.

Paul was thoroughly enjoying life in the fast lane, and although it seemed that he was devoted to Jane Asher, his attention could be easily distracted by another star who happened to be present during their nights out in the fashionable and expensive houses and eateries in London.

For the moment, John even seemed to enjoy life as a stay-at-home husband and father to Julian, who had been born in April 1963.

The film plot for Help! was ludicrous, based around a sacred ruby ring wanted by a religious cult, which forces the Fab Four to go running through some exotic locations in Europe and the Bahamas. It served, as did the first film, as a vehicle for their songs. But what songs they were; 'Ticket to Ride', 'You've Got to Hide Your Love Away', 'Help!', and one of the most covered and beautiful pop songs ever, 'Yesterday'.

The film came out on the 29th of July 1965; one review will suffice. "... a failure, for as actors they are still nothing

48

NEWS FLASH!
NEW BEATLES SINGLE

FOR RELEASE ON APRIL 9

+++++ For release April 9 on EMI's PARLOPHONE label
new BEATLES single

TICKET TO RIDE and YES IT IS

+++++ Both titles are LENNON-McCARTNEY compositions, both will be included in THE BEATLES NEW FILM.

+++++ "TICKET TO RIDE", a fastish number features JOHN and PAUL singing, with JOHN taking the lead.

+++++ "YES IT IS" is slow and in three-part harmony (JOHN, PAUL and GEORGE), with JOHN again taking the lead.

+++++ PARLOPHONE R 5265

A WALTER SH SUBRAFI Product

Press Release for "Ticket To Ride"   *Filming of 'Help!', Obertauern, Austria, 1965*

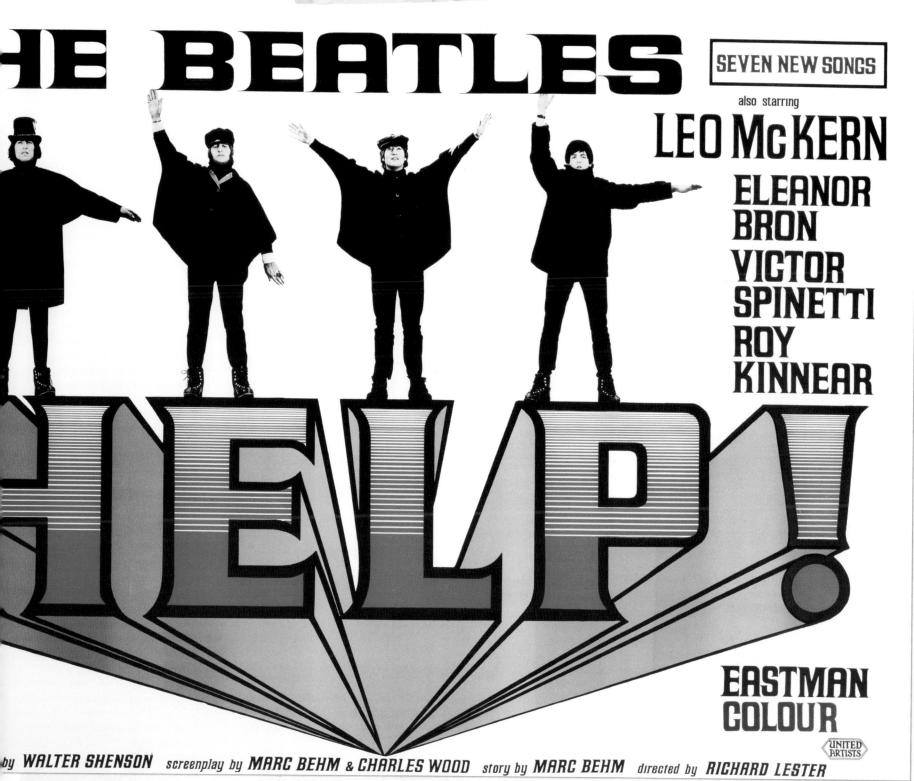

British Poster of Richard Lester's 'Help!'

but Beatles, without enough characterisation—or even caricaturisation—to play anything but sight gags."

Nonetheless, there were comparisons to the Marx Brothers, and Ringo was singled out for particular praise.

By that time, though, the Beatles knew that they were going to be awarded MBEs, a fact which rather bemused them as they didn't think that playing rock and roll music was sufficient reason to make someone eligible. But this was the start of a new era, pop groups and 'celebrities' would be exploited by politicians who wished to garner the votes of their huge fan bases; the swinging 60s were underway, and not only The Beatles' lives were changing.

Staid, worthy old London town exploded into youthful colour, with short skirts, hipster trousers and anything you could find in the King's Road, "an endless frieze of mini-skirted, booted, fair-haired angular angels", or Carnaby Street, adorning a breakout generation of young people; and if the model Jean Shrimpton was the Queen of this young and audacious rainbow kingdom then the Beatles were certainly the kings. And when young people spoke about music, the big question was "Are you Beatles or are you Stones?", because the Stones, too, were riding high on the waves of music success. And the two bands were great friends, all rivalry produced for publicity purposes.

The album for Help!, the group's fifth UK album, was finally released in August 1965. Produced by George Martin, it contained fourteen tracks and would reach number one in both the UK and the US.

Two months later, in October, the crowds gathered once again as the Beatles turned up at Buckingham Palace to receive their MBEs – much to the disgust of some other holders of the award, who returned their own decorations considering them to have been debased. To them, indeed to the Beatles themselves as they walked on the red carpet down the white and gold state ballroom towards the monarch, it must have seemed as though the time was out of joint. If Mr. Brian Epstein, non-MBE, had felt the same, no one would have blamed him. It was a hard lesson. The first night telegrams, flowers, fruit and champagne that he always made certain were there, the dedication and hard work, the unquestioning support provided by armies of assistants such as hairdressers, lawyers, doctors, tailors and so on that he marshalled on their behalf, were obviously not going to produce an MBE. Only the limelight did that.

Mr. Brian Epstein had other matters to ponder, other compensations; he had been offered millions for the sale of both The Beatles and NEMS Enterprises, now boasting hugely successful acts such as Cilla Black and Billy J. Kramer alongside The Beatles. He was, therefore, now no stranger to wealth as the art and expensive furnishings in his Georgian house in exclusive Belgravia, London, testified.

Yet The Beatles were obviously his number one concern; his feelings for John Lennon had intensified unbearably,

50

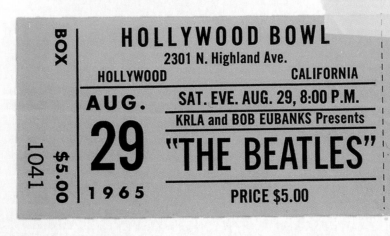

not withstanding all of John's ruthless and brutal barbs sent in his direction. An unresolvable problem; it meant that The Beatles were his raison d'être, but that Brian was never truly relaxed around them. He wanted desperately to be one of them, and if not that, then at least to be in their presence. It was a one-sided love affair that Brian would go to any lengths to preserve. If 'his' Beatles wanted to meet Elvis, then meet Elvis they would, and did, during both of their 1964 and 1965 American tours. Heads would roll if Brian felt that anyone was getting closer to The Beatles than they should. His jealous cruelty could then be boundless. The band, according to American lawyer Nat Weiss, who became a confidante to Brian, was more like a vocation in his life or a religion, men with whom he

imagined he was connected in an almost mystical fashion. Perhaps they were more responsible than any other one factor for his Jekyll and Hyde character. His naivety in financial matters was based on his past rooted in the caution of the Liverpool retail trade. One result of this was that the 1964 American tour only broke even, and the merchandising side of his business slewed out of control, so that everyone ended up in rancorous lawsuits, battles that also cost tens of millions of dollars in lost revenue.

Even worse was that Brian was losing interest in his other protégés, whilst continuing to sign singers who had no chance of success in the mistaken belief that he had the Midas touch. The foundations of NEMS were beginning to weaken

51

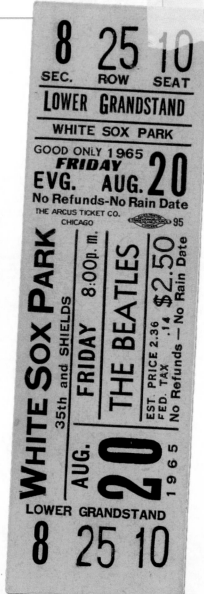

Police struggle to hold the line of Beatles fans at Buckingham Palace

dangerously. And surrounded by luxury, King Brian Midas was beginning to lose contact with reality. Neither had success done anything to reduce the blind fear that the 'rough trade' he preferred, would lead to his being 'discovered', or blackmailed – or worse, that the Beatles would find out; as though they didn't know. He was sinking into emotional quicksand.

Two of The Beatles, at least, were far more concerned about conflict closer to home.

John and Paul were two songwriters whose contrasting characters produced songs that made The Beatles unique. If the album Help! had shown this to be true, the album they recorded and released in 1965, Rubber Soul, brought this dichotomy to the fore. McCartney was a far more natural musician, more disciplined, more constrained, gentler in his attitudes despite his love of rock 'n' roll. John, in contrast, cynical, aggressive and loathing constraint in any form, was the antidote that injected energy and sharpness into songs which then breathed harmony to the listeners but were born of a dogged, competitive collaboration. The two musicians' jagged edges meant that their lives now only joined, if necessary, for professional reasons. The new album was one such reason.

Produced over several weeks in Abbey Road with four-track recording, Rubber Soul was a folk-rock album that also incorporated pop and soul elements; the second album to contain all original material. This was the Beatles as mature songwriters, and their musical tapestry was more expressive, involving harmonium, sitars and fuzz bass with brighter tones for the guitar. The Beatles' persistent demands led to changes in studio recording techniques. For the first time, they were viewing the album form as an artistic project, an idea that influenced the way pop bands viewed albums from then on. Two standout songs, 'Michelle', by Paul McCartney, and 'Nowhere Man' by John Lennon, demonstrate the different approaches by the songwriters and the widening rift between them musically and personally.

The ballad 'Michelle' was born because McCartney wanted to write something with a melody and a bass line in it. Perhaps reflecting his peaceful life and love affair with Jane Asher. It was a unique Beatles song, in that it was partly in French; it harked back to

Paul's Liverpool days when the Parisian left bank intellectuals were à la mode. It was a French teacher who came up with the phrase "Michelle ma belle", and Lennon who suggested the bridge, "I love you". It became a Grammy Award winner.

John Lennon's 'Nowhere Man', on the other hand, was written almost from desperation when Lennon needed another song for the album, but the seesawing refrain and dissonant chords are not only an indication of his state of mind, but of the increasingly philosophical direction of his thinking in his work. McCartney thought that this song was what John would come up at dawn after a night out. "I think at that point… (John was) wondering where he was going, and to be truthful so was I. I was starting to worry about him."

Apart from learning the sitar, George was also writing songs, but by himself, and one of them usually found its way onto a Beatles album. Although he would lend his vocals to harmonies, he never seemed quite at ease doing so and always appeared slightly apart from the two frontmen. Much like the more placid and optimistic Ringo, who was happy doing whatever George Martin wanted and able to relax when not needed.

In 1966, the times they were a-changing – especially for George, who married Pattie Boyd on the 21st of January 1966 – and pop musicians, tiring of the anodyne love story, were lurching into protest songs. Although The Beatles were apolitical, they, too, were moving into pastures new as two new songs proved; Paul's 'Paperback Writer', released early in 1966 with its criticism of journalism and mass media, in tandem with John's 'Rain', hitting out at the relentless pressure he felt subjected to. The single went to number one in both Britain and America, an America now submerged, to the consternation of parents and establishment, in the British Invasion.

There were, of course, touring commitments to fulfill; the UK in the winter of 1965 and the European and world tour of 1966. The UK tour was memorable for the concert in Liverpool, which was their sixth, but turned out to be the last. A nostalgic event, for the Cavern Club, too, would soon be relegated to the past, giving way to a car park. There was reason for reminiscence in Europe when they visited Hamburg and met old friends from their

52

Teenagers hold a 'Bang the Beatles' protest where they are burning records, books, and wigs due to remarks made by John Lennon

53

Reeperbahn days. There was a thoughtful reunion with Astrid Kirchherr, who had given up photography, finding resistance to female photographers in the 60s too difficult to overcome. There was still a picture of Stu Sutcliffe on the wall.

Perhaps all of these thought-provoking, reflective moments helped create a wall of discontent that no one except the lads' closest confidantes would have seen growing in height. The discontent reached its zenith on the Philippines leg of the tour. Having failed to attend a party given by Mrs. Imelda Marcos, wife of the brutal dictator of the Philippines, Ferdinand Marcos, there was a "Beatles snub president" headline next morning, which led to them being verbally and physically abused on their way to the plane. It was the final straw. Back in London, they decided to call it quits. Brian's world disintegrated in front of his eyes.

There was barely time to consider his feelings, however, because

one of John's infamous remarks had also exploded onto the world stage. It had lain dormant for many months before being revived prior to the Beatles' tour of America in August. By which time it had done its worst.

"Christianity will go. It will vanish and shrink... We're more popular than Jesus now..."; and for good measure, John had also decided that the disciples were "thick".

Liberal Britain just laughed.

Religious America's jaw dropped.

The results made the Philippines experience seem like a day at the fair. "Place Beatle trash here" bins appeared in the USA, and 35 US radio stations banned their music. And just to help matters along a little, Capitol Records issued an album of tracks from Help! and Rubber Soul, with a sleeve boasting The

I'M 4 'S

Beatles wearing white smocks and holding bloody pieces of meat and decapitated dolls. The effect was instantaneous leading to horrified radio DJs and a new cover in double quick time. The "Butcher sleeve" had been John's idea, of course; bitterly resentful at its withdrawal, he said the graphic was as relevant as Vietnam. John's one-man vitriolic acid attack against the world spread rapidly from pulpit to pulpit, from Africa to South America.

In England no one took much notice, because now, on the heels of the British invasion of America, London was swinging, the capital of culture, and the Americans were coming over to see what the upstart town was all about; after all, a town that harboured The Beatles must have something special. And The Beatles had something special for them just before they themselves went on tour in the US.

Revolver, an album they had been recording between April and June that year of 1966, was released on the 5th of August. The lads had been more friendly with one another during its inception than they had been for a long time, although one argument between McCartney and his bandmates led to him walking out of the studio on the 21st of June during the final session for 'She Said She Said'. Ringo described the sessions well: "We were really starting to find ourselves in the studio... finding what we could do... The overdubbing got better, even though it was always pretty tricky because of the lack of tracks. The songs got more interesting, so with that the effects got more interesting."

With the album containing songs such as 'Eleanor Rigby', 'Love You To', 'Yellow Submarine, 'She Said She Said', 'Good Day Sunshine', 'Got to Get You into My Life' and 'Tomorrow Never Knows', from love songs to drug songs, it was a remarkable collection, encapsulating swinging London.

This was The Beatles coming of age, with sophisticated use of studio techniques and effects and with a little help from some friendly substances; "...I think the drugs were kicking in a little more heavily on this album. I don't think we were on anything major yet; just the old usual – the grass

and the acid...", said Ringo. This was the band moving in a new direction, their themes touching on death, dreams and metaphysical transcendence. This, as one author wrote, was The Beatles challenging "...all the conventions of pop" with a mix of novel sounds and more complex themes for the songs. The album also confirmed that Paul McCartney was maturing into The Beatles' songwriter par excellence, and this was nowhere more evident than in 'Eleanor Rigby', 'For No One' and 'Here, There And Everywhere', which must count as three of his best songs ever, proving him to be a consummate writer of ballads.

Whereas Rubber Soul was folk and R&B oriented, Revolver saw a veritable fireworks display of influences, incorporating elements of R&B, raga rock, Motown, children's songs, chamber music, acid rock, classical Indian music and musique concrète.

'Eleanor Rigby', a song that together with Harrison's 'Taxman' set the intense tone for the album, has been described as a "narrative about the perils of loneliness", about "sermons that no one will hear". Whilst its lyrics arose from the combined efforts of the entire group, Lennon and Harrison supplied harmonies to McCartney's lead vocal, but none of them played, the musical accompaniment being provided by a string octet with arrangements by George Martin.

'Tomorrow Never Knows' was, perhaps, the most innovative song on an album full of probing musical, technical and thematic curiosity. It represented an enormous progression for the band, incorporating lyrics adapted from Timothy Leary's A Manuel Based on the Tibetan Book of the Dead, equating meditation and LSD 'enlightenment', and a thunderous drum sound. Lennon wanted a Buddhist ceremony ambience. One of the ways he achieved this was in the song's harmonic structure, which was based on Indian music and revolved around a high-volume C drone from George Harrison's tambura.

Innovative use of tape loops and Leslie speakers went hand in hand with artificial double tracking, or ADT, which

54

Press conference on August 6, 1966 in New York

55

employed two linked tape recorders to create a doubled vocal track. The minute differences in playback meant that the recordings would separated slightly, leaving an impression of two voices when combined. A by-product of this was that recordings could be sped up or slowed down, a technique The Beatles used extensively on the album.

"We were really hard workers. That's another thing about The Beatles – we worked like dogs to get it right", Ringo said.

Their hard days' night certainly paid off. The UK reviewers were full of praise: "Full of musical ingenuity... there are parts that will split the pop fraternity neatly down the middle." Another effused that this was an album that would "change the direction of pop music".

To Brian, the album's success must now have seemed like a Pyrrhic victory. Also, he was so worried when he arrived in America for the next tour that he proposed cancelling the tour, paying $1 million of his own money to do so, rather than have The Beatles at risk from physical abuse. Or worse. As they set off on their nineteen shows, shuttling around the vast continent, a clairvoyant predicted that they would all die in an air crash. Which made for very relaxed flying during the entire tour; one which had been given the worst send off all ever.

It also ended up being the last ever.

John was forced into an apology for his Jesus remark, perhaps made more contrite by the volume of hate mail he had received in the US, sincerely telling a Chicago press conference, "I'm sorry I opened my mouth". Nonetheless, the remark followed him and plagued him in press conferences around America. From baton-swinging police attacking audiences, to race riots, to ugly scenes when an open-air concert had to be abandoned because of the rain, the tour reached peak fear in Memphis where the Klu Klux Klan had threatened them and where rubbish was thrown onto the stage. When a firecracker went off, the band thought a gun had been fired. Brian had money and incriminating photos and letters stolen and was so overwhelmed with the potential blackmail scenario that he didn't dare even leave the house.

So on the 29th of August 1966, the Beatles' still besotted manager missed the last commercial live concert the Beatles ever gave; something he never forgave himself for.

It was a more poignant event than he knew, because for the man who had groomed the Liverpool lads for stardom, time was running out.

56

Police clear the field of enthusiastic fans as The Beatles perform on a bandstand in Candlestick Park, San Francisco, California

57

TUES. EVE., AUG. 23, at 7:30 P.M.

SID BERNSTEIN presents

THE BEATLES
IN PERSON!

plus

THE CYRKLE · THE RONETTES · THE REMAINS · BOBBY HEBB

at SHEA STADIUM

TICKETS BY MAIL: $4.50, $5.00, $5.75 (tax incl.) add 50¢ to each order for cost of mailing. Make check or money orders payable to:

Tickets also available at
SINGER CENTER (RECORD DEPT.)
Rockefeller Center Promenade
Fifth Ave., bet. 49th & 50th St.

SID BERNSTEIN
ENTERPRISES, INC.
1180 6th Ave., N.Y., N.Y.
10036

INFORMATION: 212 265-2280

*Poster and Ticket for the
Shea Stadium Gig*

SEC. 44 R ROW 9 SEAT
UPPER RESERVED

SHEA STADIUM
FLUSHING, N.Y.

TUESDAY
AUG.
23
1966
7:30 P.M.

SID BERNSTEIN, Presents
"THE BEATLES"

PRICE $5.75
PERFORMANCE HELD
RAIN OR SHINE

SID BERNSTEIN, Presents

NO REFUNDS — NO EXCHANGES

SEC. 44 R ROW 9 SEAT
UPPER RESERVED

SHEA STADIUM
ENTER GATE A
TUE., AUG. 23, 1966-7:30 P.M.
$5.75

SUDDENLY, JUST MEMORIES

It was 1967, the year of the summer of love, a year that would change everything for The Beatles. With more fame and money then anyone could handle whirring around them at such young ages, it would have been a miracle if four young men had come through their dreams come true completely unscathed. The cracks within the group were already widening into rifts, and as the merry-go-round slowed down enough for the lads to think more clearly, with a three-month recording pause after the tour in 1966, it was John Lennon who broke ranks first.

His talent for acting had been noticed in Help!, and now he proved his mentor, director Richard Lester, correct in How I won the War, which was released in October 1967 with praise for Lennon's performance as Musketeer Gripweed. But he found filming too easy to want to repeat the experience, from which he took away, and retained from then on, cropped hair and round school-master spectacles.

Although he often seemed to fall into lethargy that year, there was another radical change waiting for him; two versions of their meeting exist, but whichever is correct, by the end of 1966, after Lennon had visited a conceptual art exhibit in the Indica Gallery in London, he had a fatal meeting; fatal for the Beatles, that is. He was introduced to Yoko Ono.

In contrast, Ringo seemed happy to stay at home with his wife and new baby Zak, whereas Paul and George also found themselves facing an unwelcome hiatus in their lives, which they were not quite sure how to fill. They had everything money could buy, but were left with an uneasy sense of dissatisfaction; yes, even Paul, despite his wealthy life in London with the lovely Jane Asher.

George had become so disillusioned that he had to be persuaded not to leave the group but soon after, he found another anchor in his life.

George had already begun to enjoy playing the sitar, an instrument that gave him a newfound confidence within the group and had even taken lessons with the famous sitar player Ravi Shankar. Now he devoted every spare minute day and night to mastering the instrument. Also, George's wife, Pattie Boyd, was interested in Eastern mysticism; she belonged to the Spiritual Regeneration Movement, and encouraged The Beatles to meet Maharishi Mahesh Yogi, an Indian mystic, in London in August 1967. George was the most interested, and he and Pattie travelled to Kashmir, where they talked to holy men and their students and watched religious festivals. George read books about meditation and yoga, Hindu philosophy and about enlightenment and peace, which helped him put the rigours of being a Beatle into perspective.

Less fortunately, he was now a regular user of LSD, which seemed to replicate the brilliant sights, sounds and colours of India.

Brian had made himself scarce. He had bought the Saville Theatre in London and now played at being a theatrical impresario. He even directed a play at London's New Arts Theatre, and looked to find a partner for NEMS Enterprises. The word amongst those in the know was that he was depressed. No one took much notice, although, of course, with his track record, they should have. He was heavily using the drug carbromal, an hypnotic drug, a barbiturate-like sedative. During the months when The Beatles were involved in recording sessions for a new album, Epstein was now either on holiday, or at the Priory Clinic in Putney, attempting to get his drug use under control. He was in despair at his life, at what he saw as his inability to have intimate relationships, with males or females, and he knew that the deep bond with The Beatles, his raison d'être, had been irretrievably broken.

Early in the New Year of 1967, Brian tried to kill himself. Again.

He was saved from the drug overdose, as he had been late

59

Brian Epstein at his Saville Theatre, where seats were broken during a Chuck Berry concert

Press launch for newly completed album, 'Sergeant Pepper's', held at manager Brian Epstein's house, 1967

in 1966 when he had made his first attempt, thwarted on that occasion by his secretary and chauffeur.

By then, the band had already begun work on their new album at EMI studios in London, a project that would see them recording until the 21st of April 1967.

Impatient with the long months without a new Beatle product to sell, Parlophone were happy to be squeeze a single out of the lads with 'Penny Lane' and 'Strawberry Fields Forever' on either side, both of which had been intended for the album. It was released on the 17th of February 1967. 'Penny Lane' was mostly written by Paul, whereas 'Strawberry Fields', the name of a Salvation Army children's home in Liverpool, was John's baby. It contrasted vividly with Paul's song in that John had poured many elements of his character into it, from the philosophical to the sarcastic, from the surreal to the despairing.

Paul had chosen to depict suburban skies over a suburban street, overlaid with a surrealist veneer that evoked an idealised Liverpool of the past. Innovative, again, was the use of the piccolo trumpet, something never used in a pop song before, and McCartney's complex tonal changes from verse to chorus. As ever, George Martin's arrangements were superb.

It was also in the month of February, following the recording sessions for the song "Sgt. Pepper's Lonely Hearts Club Band", that Paul McCartney's idea for an album performed by the fictional Sgt. Pepper band was discussed. The finished product would be spoken of by musicologists as the first concept album, heralding the era of the concept album and art rock. The Beatles threw everything at it; Indian classical music, western classical music, avant-garde, circus, musical, vaudeville. It was destined for extraordinary admiration, lauded as "the most important and influential rock and roll album ever recorded", one that opened the gates for the many genres of pop music that followed.

60

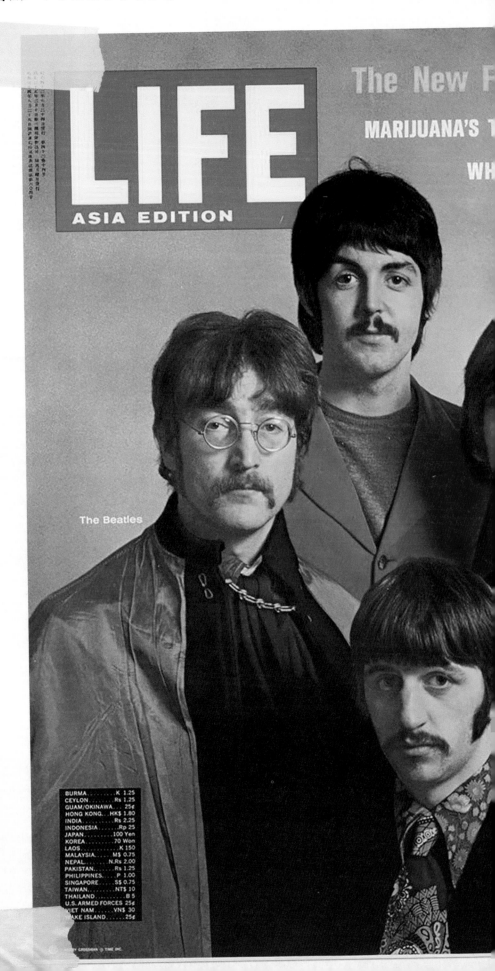

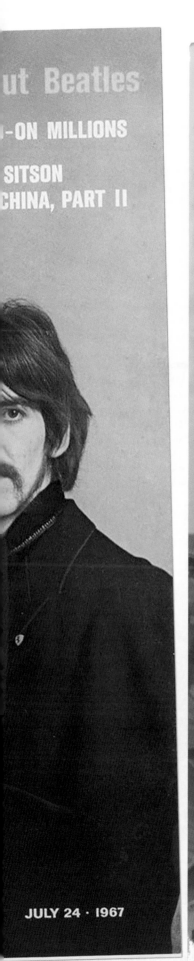

ut Beatles

-ON MILLIONS

SITSON
CHINA, PART II

JULY 24 · 1967

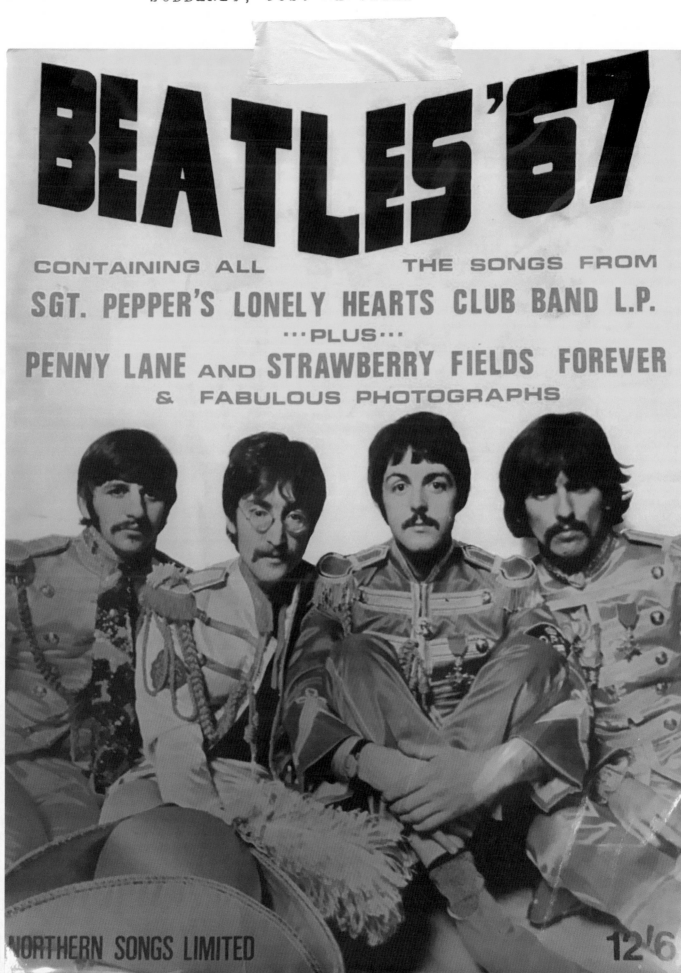

61

With a little help from their friend LSD, which even McCartney had succumbed to, the four lads resumed the closeness they had once had – even sprouting four identical moustaches to prove it – and produced scintillating music and outstanding performances. George was happy enough, even though his heart was still in India and he was fed up with being one of the Fab Four, as he confessed later; for his song 'Within You, Without You' his sitar was accompanied by Indian musicians.

John and Paul excelled themselves.

'A Day in the Life' was a tight collaboration between them, banned by the BBC for fear it was alluding to recreational drug use. It acquired the tag, a "marijuana dream", a nickname helped by the vocal wailing that panned from left to right. Brass and orchestra brought volume to the crescendos, an idea by McCartney. This song, with its cross fades and technical experimentation, has been said to depict disillusionment with life and has been spoken of in extraordinary terms as "...among the most penetrating and innovative artistic reflections of its era... (The Beatles) finest single achievement".

Despite the artistic success of the album, John was beginning to succumb to resentment, feeling that he was just producing songs on demand, which didn't allow him to scoop deeply enough into the well of his own creative visions. And once again, Paul's domination of the album was apparent, an album filled with treasures such as 'With a Little Help from My Friends', 'Lucy in the Sky with Diamonds', 'She's Leaving Home', 'When I'm Sixty-Four', 'Lovely Rita', or 'Good Morning Good Morning'. Lucy, of course, came in for a good deal of attention, and the widespread suspicion that she was on an LSD trip was hard to dispel, despite both Lennon and McCartney insisting that the title name was coincidental and invented by John's son Julian; although, said Paul, the lyrics were intended to be psychedelic. The powerful imagery of "tangerine trees" and "marmalade skies", combined with Lennon's almost child-like voice and McCartney's Lowrey organ, producing an effect Martin

found mesmerising, introduced a song that was a heady mix of Alice in Wonderland meets rock and roll.

Then, topping the album off in spectacular style was a forty-one-piece orchestra, whose musicians had no musical notation to play from, but who were instructed to achieve John's crescendo announcing the "end of the world".

(Once Sgt. Pepper had been released and all The Beatles, including 'squeaky-clean' Paul and Brian, confessed to taking LSD before it had been made illegal, the squeals of horror could be heard from London's Daily Mail to America's Dr. Billy Graham... and even in Elvis's house; perhaps his own vast intake of prescription drugs made him particularly sensitive.)

Sgt. Pepper's Lonely Hearts Club Band was the band's eighth studio album. It hit the shops on the 1st of June 1967, and immediately powered up to the top of the charts, lingering for 27 weeks at the top of the UK album chart and 15 weeks at the top in the US. Critics acknowledged its innovations in music production, songwriting and graphic design, which linked pop music to legitimate art and gave musical form to 1960s counterculture. Four Grammy Awards came its way in 1968, one of which was Album of the Year, the first rock LP to receive the honour.

Sgt. Pepper embodied "the social, the musical, and more generally, the cultural changes of the 1960s" enthused one musicologist. The Times went even further with "a decisive moment in the history of Western civilisation". No less. It contained, it seemed, music for everyone from the young to the old, to the pothead, to the dreamer, to the philosopher. Newsweek said it was a "masterpiece", and John must have been delighted when "A Day in the Life" was compared to Eliot's The Waste Land.

There was not only praise; "however, dazzling...ultimately fraudulent", said another reviewer, and in later years came "if not the worst, then certainly the most overrated album of all time".

STEREO

63

The classic Sgt. Pepper's Lonely Hearts Club Band cover
created by Jann Haworth and Peter Blake

After the album launch party at his house, Brian returned to the Priory immediately.

The Beatles soon bestowed upon the world another song, destined to become a 60s anthem; 'All You Need Is Love', which was broadcast to TV networks in 31 countries via the BBC's embrace of satellite technology.

There wasn't much love around from the police that year, who conducted an all-out assault on druggies everywhere. And one event seemed to symbolize the fact that love was turning into vileness and jealousy; the playwright Joe Orton was beaten to death by Kenneth Halliwell, his lover, who then took his own life. This happened in August 1967. For The Beatles, the deaths turned out to be the supporting acts to a devastating event in their own lives.

October 1967 would see the five-year management contract Brian Epstein had negotiated with The Beatles come to an end, and in Brian's overwrought imagination, they would not seek to renew it. As Cilla Black had told him in the summer that she intended to leave NEMS Enterprises, he was filled with foreboding, despite eventually persuading her to stay with him. But nothing could dissuade him from his conviction that The Beatles were leaving him.

He was not wrong in feeling uneasy; Paul, especially, was not happy with the way Brian was conducting business. The mistakes about the merchandising had filtered through, and talk of a massive advance of $1.25 million paid to the Stones, gave rise to The Beatles questioning whether Brian was still the man they should have in charge of their affairs.

Now, too, Brian's father had died. Brian spent time at home with his mother in Liverpool and attended the traditional Jewish shiva, before she came to stay with him for ten days in London. He seemed content and at ease when his mother left to return to Liverpool on the 24th of August.

On the 25th of August, The Beatles were in Bangor in Wales to attend the Maharishi's Transcendental Meditation retreat.

Two days later, in his locked bedroom, Brian died of an overdose of Cabitral, a type of sleeping pill, six of which, together with alcohol, had finally relieved him of the pain of living. He was 32 years old.

The Beatles were still in Wales when Peter Brown, Brian's assistant, phoned them with the devastating news. Rumour suggested suicide, although the coroner ruled that the death was accidental.

George Harrison's wife, Pattie, recalled that both Paul and George went into complete shock. Brian, Pattie added, "… had found them, believed in them, moulded them, turned them into millionaires, and made them famous the world over". Understandable, then, that his demise found the group "… disoriented and fearful about the future". John Lennon, too, had heard the sound of a door slamming closed; "We collapsed. I knew that we were in trouble then. I didn't really have any misconceptions about our ability to do anything other than play music, and I was scared. I thought, we've had it now".

Thirty years later, Paul McCartney said in an interview that "If anyone was the Fifth Beatle, it was Brian… Brian would really be happy to hear how much we loved him".

Indeed he would have been, but the sentiment came, perhaps, thirty years too late.

Unlike the Maharishi's, who considered death was "not important"; the sight of The Beatles' ravaged faces as they left the retreat in Wales to return to London convinced everyone that they did not feel the same.

As a painful after note to Brian's death, a murder theory arose that harked back to tens and tens of millions of dollars lost during the merchandise fiasco – and the death by hanging of Brian's solicitor, David Jacobs, a year later did nothing to quell the whispers.

64

The Beatles with the Maharishi Mahesh Yogi, 1967

The Beatles and their wives at the Rishikesh in India with the Maharishi Mahesh Yogi, March 1968

WHERE HAVE ALL THE COLOURS GONE?

In the hiatus following Brian's death, The Beatles slipped into a new era, and despite the Maharishi's death pronouncement, they became full members of the Spiritual Regeneration Movement, which meant they were to pay one week's earnings per month for the privilege and had to visit his Academy in India.

Brian's brother Clive took over at NEMS. Brian's partner, Robert Stigwood, who the Beatles disliked, was bought out.

It was the ever-resourceful Paul who showed the steps up into the immediate future through the confusion of the present, coming up with the concept that was interesting enough to cause the group to cancel their planned visit to Maharishi.

Ever since the end of the recording sessions for Sgt. Pepper, McCartney had been mulling over another idea; it was based on a song he'd written that hadn't made it onto the Sgt. Pepper album and was called 'Magical Mystery Tour'. Now, he put to the others the idea of a bus tour around the British seaside towns, seeing what surprises could be elicited from the English countryside; his idea fell into amenable ears. Cameras would follow them around, but the lads would be in charge of directing them. So, in September 1967 a coach emblazoned with Magical Mystery Tour on its sides set off into the unknown British countryside, with no script, and 43 assorted actors, journalists, midgets and a fat lady on board - to encounter an optimism-deflating confusion of non-booked hotels,

no mystery, no magic and hardly any humour. Certainly not when they got stuck on narrow bridges. It all ended on a disused airfield with 40 dwarfs and a military band; amongst other things too numerous to mention.

The confusion continued through to the editing in which the Beatles all 'helped' - at different times, re-editing what the others had already edited. Reconvened at Abbey Road Studios, they recorded the soundtrack, which produced perhaps one of the daftest Beatles songs of all time, which, of course, went to number one in Britain and America; 'Hello, Goodbye'. Mystery Tour's 52 minutes were shown on BBC TV on Boxing Day 1967.

The show was panned. The sight of The Beatles either dressed up in bad animal costumes for 'I Am the Walrus', George repeating 29 times "don't be long", or the Fab Four dressed in red robes as wizards, brought forth unprecedented vitriol; "Blatant rubbish", thundered the press in a variety of ways, causing the Americans to cancel a television deal.

Although McCartney thought that it was alright, at the time he said, "It was a challenge and it didn't come off". Even George Martin confessed that it "looked awful and was a disaster".

With a touch of regret, everyone realised that such a thing could never have happened in Brian Epstein's world.

The soundtrack, on the other hand, released as an LP, went

to number one on the US Billboard top LPs chart, even though there was a lukewarm reception for most of the new songs, with opinion divided between Mystery Tour producing boring sound, typical of The Beatles of that period, or being far ahead of the madding crowd. The song 'Magical Mystery Tour' did not have "... compelling enough lyrics or sufficient melodic interest ... to rise to greatness", and McCartney's 'The Fool on the Hill' was "... the most unworthy Beatles standard since 'Michelle' ". Only George's 'Blue Jay Way', opening with a church organ leading into a "whirlpool of sound", escaped and was described as hypnotic.

December 1967 was a busy month for The Beatles, because they also opened their Apple boutique that month, one of many attempts, now increasing in number, to evade the taxman's 90% grasp. Expensively stocked with exotic, colourful oriental fabrics and glittering jewellery – all brought in by design group The Fool, who also conceptualised the interiors – and staffed with some of some of the prettiest girls in London, Apple flung its doors wide open on the 7th of September 1967. The name spawned an empire that mushroomed above the boutique and included Apple Music, Apple Records, Apple Publicity, Apple Retail, Apple Films and Apple Electronics. This empire was the tangible evidence that finally, The Beatles had taken control of their own business interests. Early in new year of 1968, Apple Corps Ltd. appeared, its sparkling offices in Wigmore Street. The only thing the lads didn't seem to be in control of was the new executives' blossoming salaries.

Hopeful, maybe, of attracting some of that Apple Corps wealth was a man in India named Maharishi Mahesh Yogi, to whose ashram the four betook themselves in February 1968 for three months. Not an ascetic ashram by any means; there was running water and English furniture in stone bungalows with telephones and food in abundance. They reminded Ringo of a Butlins holiday camp and became the backdrop for George's 25th birthday. The honoured guests were even allowed the odd illicit bottle of wine. The four Liverpool lads donned their best hippy attire and sat cross-legged at the guru's feet beside such other luminaries

as Mia Farrow and English folk star Donovan.

Ringo had soon had enough of chanting, mass prayer and fasting and was gone ten days later leaving Maureen behind. The others, still with their girlfriends Jane, Pattie and John's wife Cynthia, engaged in meditation competitions – Paul won with four hours –also taking the opportunity of being unmolested to write new songs.

They made it to nine weeks. Then Paul and Jane decided that they'd had enough, too. John was still waiting for the penny

Paul McCartney at the start of 'Magical Mystery Tour'

MAGICAL MYSTERY TOUR

THE FOOL ON THE HILL I AM THE WALRUS
FLYING BLUE DAY WAY
YOUR MOTHER SHOULD KNOW

68

STARRING "THE BEATLES"

FILMED IN ENGLAND by The Beatles, written by The Beatles
Music Composed by The Beatles

LONDON DAILY EXPRESS . . ."Blatant Rubbish . . .
. . . Tasteless Nonsense"

CARSON ENTERTAINMENT GROUP

1145 Willora Rd. — Stockton, Calif. 95207
(209) 478-3816

to drop containing the wisdom of ages; the penny did drop;
but it wasn't the one that John had expected and began
its descent with the rumour that the Maharishi was not
quite genuine. Not quite not of this world. Also, John was
developing a growing interest in Mia Farrow. He, George
and a disappointed Cynthia, were going home.

And that was it.

"We made a mistake", said Paul.

It was time to return to more interesting, material,
considerations. Only George pursued his spiritual
interests back in England.

And business it was, rather than music that consumed their
summer that year. With 'philanthropic' motives they were
going to seek out new artists and give them the freedom to
create; i.e. funds to stay alive.

Abbey Road saw the group only to record 'Hey Jude' and
some songs for the soundtrack of their third contractual
film for United Artists – which turned out to be a cartoon
feature film, much to their relief, with actors imitating
their voices. They put little effort into the soundtrack,
either, creating just four unreleased songs; 'Only a
Northern Song' (a song showing how little The Beatles cared
about the soundtrack; it's George's lyrical complaint at
being nothing more than a songwriter under contract to
Northern Songs, The Beatles' publishing company) and 'It's
too Much', were both proclaimed by Beat Instrumental as
being "superb pieces", and were from George Harrison's pen,
and 'Hey Bulldog' and 'Altogether Now' were by Lennon and
McCartney. 'Yellow Submarine' and 'All You Need is Love'
rounded off the Beatles' contributions. In later years,
'Hey Bulldog' a "tough and funky piano-driven rocker", did
attract praise, considered as by far "the best of the new
songs". George Martin was forced to write an orchestral
score for side two.

So, great was the surprise when the film, Yellow Submarine,

was released in July 1968 to critical acclaim for its "Lush, wildly creative images", with George mentioning that the actors brought a certain character to the film that the group themselves would not have been able to. The animated musical fantasy comedy was even credited with awakening interest in animation as a serious art form.

The only one who gained much from their visit to India was George, whose soundtrack to the film Wonderwall, provided Wonderwall Music, his debut solo album. A great deal of it had been recorded in Bombay in January 1968 and featured the Indian classical musicians Aashish Khan, Shankar Ghosh and Shivkumar Sharma.

There were more serious events at 94 Baker Street, the Apple boutique. Not only had the local council objected to the psychedelic mural outside and asked for it to be removed, everyone, including the employees, seemed to have their hand in the till in one way or another and shoplifting by customers was rife. The group pulled the plug on the pandemonium at the end of July.

Our main business, said McCartney, "is entertainment and communication", to which they returned immediately to record 'Hey Jude'. All seven minutes eleven seconds of the single were sent out into the world on the 26th of August 1968. One reviewer's analysis of the song later described it as a compositional lesson in how to cover a large musical canvas with simple strokes, and combine orchestration, harmony and a bass line to "articulate form and contrast".

The song was born of a sad event; in May of that year, John and Cynthia had separated. Cynthia's famous husband suffered from bouts of depression, rendering his behaviour extremely erratic, and she and their son Julian now spent more time apart from him than with him. John's jealousy of Cynthia had faded to indifference. But it was John's affair with Yoko Ono that had overwhelmed their relationship when she had walked in on them together in her own home. Nonetheless, he fully intended to divorce Cynthia and accuse her of adultery.

After that, he refused to talk to her personally about what

John Lennon during filming of Magical Mystery Tour

69

was going to happen, and she had to make an appointment at the Apple offices – when, of course, Yoko Ono would be present.

Unable to simply break with a woman who had been an integral part of his circle of friends for so long, finding it "a bit much for them suddenly to be personae non grata and out of my life", Paul went to visit Cynthia and Julian. In the car, on the way there, he composed 'Hey Jude'. Originally entitled 'Hey Jules', it was a song of encouragement for young Julian from a concerned Paul. This song was recorded as part of what would commonly be known as "The White Album", and it was during these recording sessions that Paul's discontent at Yoko Ono's now constant presence at the microphone beside John, grew daily more dangerous.

John, despite telling Yoko that she was "like a mate", had now transferred his fierce jealousy to her, preventing her even from reading Japanese newspapers or books because the language was somewhere for her to be without him. But she became the mother figure for him, the supporter for his damaged ego, encouraged him to pursue his art, and provided a safe haven in this confusing life where his wealth and rebellious nature refused to submit to a 'bed-in' together, as they refused to do for so many successful rock 'n' roll artists.

But 'Hey Jude' also had a sad significance for Paul. Despite his affairs, Paul had enjoyed being part of Jane Asher's family, in whose reflected establishment ambience he bathed. But after five years, it seemed, the attraction had waned. He was about to turn a personal corner.

In May of 1967, Paul had been introduced to a woman who was a professional photographer of celebrities and musicians. She was unpretentiously rebellious, a free spirit and an artist who shared McCartney's love of nature. They met again exactly one year later in New York and spent the night together. From that moment on, just as John had done, Paul had found the missing piece of puzzle in his life; her name was Linda Eastman.

Now Paul, too, had someone at his side on whom he could absolutely rely, his rock in a storm, who was fiercely loyal. And she idolised him. Linda's relaxed attitude to life rubbed off on Paul; he paid less attention to his clothes, for example, would not shave and wore an old overcoat. With Linda, he realised that he was allowed to display human weaknesses, and Linda's young daughter Heather got on like a house on fire with Paul, who had always wanted children of his own; Paul would read her bedtime stories, draw cartoons for her and sing her to sleep.

Whatever the personal motivation for 'Hey Jude', it went to number one in twenty-one countries, and its 40-piece orchestral accompaniment, garnered high praise; "a beautiful, compelling song", with an "absolutely sensational" first three minutes". It was counted amongst McCartney's "truest and most forthright love songs" according to The

Village Voice, and it had the sad honour of being the last great Beatles single aimed at the 45 rpm market.

On the 30th of May 1968, The Beatles had gathered to produce their first album for Apple, and with George entering a new phase of creativity there was ample product to choose from. So much, indeed, that it was decided to pack two LPs into a dual sleeve.

Recording, however, was not going to be fun. John brought the focus of his obsession into the studio with him; Yoko Ono. She sat between John and the others, separating them. Not a good omen.

The distancing continued as the lads worked; the Lennon and McCartney connection fractured, John disliking Paul's gentle songs and Paul finding the new Lennon direction jarring, lacking in melody and purposefully provocative. No one could fail to notice what was happening when nods replaced communication – George gave up and retreated to his personal musical island, and Ringo manfully attempted to maintain motivation, going so far as to stay away from the studio when he failed. Halfway through, he decided it was all too much and that he was resigning. It took him a week in the normal atmosphere of home life with Zak his new baby boy and Maureen to restore his sense of equilibrium. Even George Martin found the razor-blade atmosphere too much to cope with on occasion and was suddenly absent from the sessions.

The arguments never stopped and creative differences burned the entire period of the sessions from May through October as the boys thrashed out an album with songs covering a range of styles incorporating elements of ska to British blues taking in Karlheinz Stockhausen and Chuck Berry along the way. Author Philip Norman described the end result, which was, not very surprisingly, lashed by the ill-will that had been nurtured in separate corners of the studio. "One-dimensional and charmless, the playing turgid, the singing harsh and somehow vindictive", he said of the simple rock

71

Yellow Submarine poster

72

John Lennon playing guitar beside his wife, the
Japanese-born American artist and musician Yoko Ono

contributions such as 'Revolution 9' and 'Yer Blues'. Although he had more approval for Paul's professionally finished tracks, he still considered them somehow "unbalanced and incomplete". Songs such as 'Honey Pie' and 'Rocky Raccoon' were too cloying without John's acidic, dilutive input. There were few songs, 'Julia', 'Blackbird' and 'Back in the USSR' were among them, that squeezed through the infighting, emerging intact as collaborative efforts in the old style.

Perversely, through the cracks in the old Beatles' power structure, George blossomed like a rare flower on the side of a stone cliff, producing gems such as 'While My Guitar Gently Weeps' and 'Savoy Truffle', a delicious piece of rock 'n' roll

to offset the dark humour of his vegetarian banner song, 'Piggies'.

In a first for The Beatles, George persuaded Eric Clapton to play lead guitar on 'While My Guitar Gently Weeps', his playing eliciting the remark that this track was "monumental", containing an unexpected trajectory, "emotive vibrato", string bends and modal changes, and Clapton's intensely rhythmic solo producing "tonal drive" as it scaled the musical register.

On the 14th of October 1968, recording came to an end to everyone's relief, and four days later, John and a pregnant Yoko were arrested for possession of cannabis.

And John had more 'bad' news for EMI and the Apple publicity department that month; it manifested itself as Unfinished Music Number One – Two Virgins, predominantly the musical result of John and Yoko's first night together. The album's sleeve boasted a naked John and Yoko, "two slightly overweight ex-junkies" as John described them, standing side by side; guaranteed to make a lot of unpleasant things hit the fan; the prudish outrage of the age was one of them. EMI executives turned into a row of Lady Madonna's and rejected it unless it was sold draped in a paper bag. Which it then was. An idiotic solution, which probably delighted John. EMI refused to distribute it, so the job was given to Track, The Who's record label. It took John six months to persuade his fellow bandmates to go ahead with the project. The 5000 copies of Two Virgins pressed in the UK, with songs inspiringly titled 'Two Virgins No. 2', 'Two Virgins No. 3' etc., failed to help the album into the charts.

Two Virgins was released on the 11th of November and followed on the 22nd by The Beatles, which became known as The White Album, thanks to its cover; white with 'The BEATLES' embossed on it.

Most critics lost their heads; "Lennon and McCartney are the greatest songwriters since Schubert" trumpeted one review about an album that revelled in a "deluge of joyful music making". The NME raved "God Bless You, Beatles!", and the New York Times declared it "a major success". Not everyone was quite so sure; "Boring beyond belief" said another New York Times review, contending that half of the songs were "profound mediocrities'.

Whichever it was, it still went to number one in the UK and America.

One day later, Yoko Ono lost the baby.

One week on, and John pleaded guilty to possessing cannabis and was fined £150.

By this time, it wasn't only the band that was wading into quicksand; so was the Apple empire. No one really paid attention to where mounds of money went, how much expenditure went on Fortnum & Mason meals and expensive wines for the entire office, its visitors and the studio guests. Theft was on a scale that had been achieved only in the Apple boutique, with brightly clothed flower people unacquainted with anyone at Apple coming in and out of the offices bearing with them anything that wasn't nailed down. Nor were matters helped by each Beatle giving birth to projects on a whim, which then, sooner or later, 'died the death'.

Result; Apple money was flowing out like water and the four Beatles still had tax liabilities of some £600,000. Each.

There was no one in overall charge. And now, even the lads could see that the mess they had allowed their accounts to get into needed to be sorted out by a Clear-up-the-Mess Tsar.

That Tsar would soon be sweeping down on them.

19th October 1968, John Lennon and Yoko Ono, leaving court

FOR WHOM THE BELL TOLLS

Paul missed performing live. He enjoyed being a performer and the exhilaration it brought, the immediacy of an audience, and he did his best to persuade the others to go back on the road. John and Ringo let themselves be persuaded, but George was adamant: there was no way in this life that he would once again subject himself to the torment of screaming girls and secretive escapes. So a compromise was sought; an album that would not be recorded in a studio but live without an audience, no overdubbing, recorded as it happened, warts and all, just like the old days. They all concurred, got George Martin, now freelancing, back on board and gathered for rehearsals in January 1969 at Twickenham film studios.

Not exactly without an audience; Yoko was there at John's side; Linda's daughter, on occasion, and a film crew, because it had been decided that blanket media coverage – book, film etc. – was needed, and friends and admirers also arrived at different points.

In the cold and fraught atmosphere, they set about working on songs old and new, and more than a hundred were recorded. George felt that Paul was once again 'getting at him' and little more than a week after starting work, he walked out of the studio saying he was leaving the band. He wouldn't leave them in the lurch, however, and returned after he had cooled down a few days later. But they decided to move to the studio being created below the Apple offices.

It was there that The Beatles created a minor sensation. Not in the studio basement, but on the roof. Ringo Starr recalled that there had always been a plan to play live somewhere, "Oh, the Palladium or the Sahara". The decision to go to the roof was taken just days before it happened. For forty-two minutes on the 30th January 1969, they recorded – and filmed for the Let it Be documentary – five songs, bringing traffic to a standstill and a stern policeman to Apple's door. It was the last live 'concert' the Fab Four would ever make.

At Apple, they put the finishing touches to the album that would become Let it Be, an album that would contain such gems as 'Let It Be', 'The Long and Winding Road' and 'Get Back' from McCartney; this last, perhaps the best song, being the result of ad-libbing in the studio.

Even before the recording sessions for the new album were over, they had segued into recording another; Abbey Road. It was as though they knew that there might not be many more opportunities.

It turned out to be an extraordinary album and is now considered to be their best work and one of the best albums of all time.

They began work in late February, but there was soon a hiatus because Ringo Starr had commitments on a film, The Magic Christian, being filmed in April. But it was March that brought a frenzy of media activity.

Paul and a pregnant Linda were to marry on the 12th of the month. Fans, female ones, were distraught, and the news led to ugly, even violent, scenes outside Paul's house. Their marriage would last for 29 years.
Not to be outdone, John and Yoko married eight days later on Gibraltar. Their honeymoon, they announced, would be at the Amsterdam Hilton Hotel and would be a "happening", as they would spend seven days in bed. Which they did, surrounded by peace placards and a good deal of derision. Yoko had found the best performance piece she could have hoped for; John Lennon.

Things were about to get even more dramatic, for by this time, the 'Tsar' had arrived.

An American businessman named Allen Klein had stepped in to fill the gap left by Brian Epstein. He was everything that Brian was not; aggressive, money oriented and fearless. His presence was a double-edged sword, because he gained vast fortunes for his clients, the Rolling Stones amongst them, rebalanced the relationship between musicians and record companies, but favoured no one but himself and made himself extremely wealthy and one of the most powerful figures in the music industry along the way. Lawsuits and the American IRS trailed in Klein's wake, but Apple was going down the drain fast and The Beatles were going down with it to the tune of £20,000 a week.

Klein was approved by Lennon first of all, and Paul had to be outvoted by the others before Klein could clamber on board, as Paul preferred Linda's lawyer father John Eastman to be the group's champion. But Klein's promises of unimagined wealth won the day, and the internal warfare could get started for real.

Paul was not happy. By May, Klein was the Beatles' business manager, and he set about trying to disentangle the nightmarish web of inter-company relationships that Brian had allowed to get so confused. One of the first victims to be axed was Apple Electronics. One by one, Klein extricated the Beatles from NEMS, amongst others,

Performing their last live public concert on the rooftop of the Apple building for the documentary, Let It Be

bringing the lads closer to financial independence. Executive heads rolled in Apple Publishing, Apple Retail and the Apple Foundation.

The four got on with their lives – John and Yoko with their second 'bed-in', in Montréal this time as John was barred from entering the USA thanks to his drug conviction. They continued to carpet bomb the media on their peace campaign. Their album Unfinished Music No. 2 – Life with the Lions was released in May with some of the reviews resorting to swearing in contempt.

Wisely, loyally, the other Beatles refused to be drawn into any disparaging remarks about John or Yoko.

Paul was becoming increasingly unhappy about Klein, and was mentally drained from living in London, where the clot of girls outside his house were showing increasing and dangerous hatred

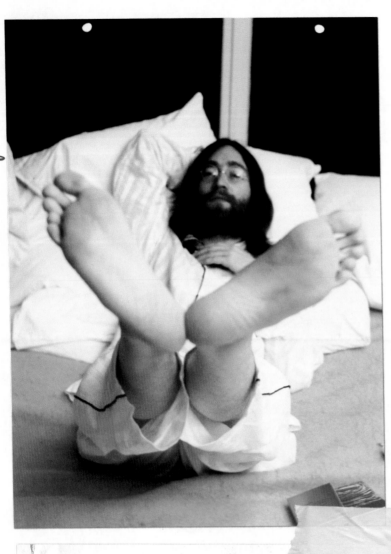

towards Linda, and he began to wish that his baby, Apple, would vanish into smoke.

His antidote was the new album Abbey Road that Paul wanted to be as it had once been when four young Liverpudlians had come together with hope in their eyes.

An extraordinary thing happened.

As the recording sessions for Abbey Road continued, which was forged into a rock album taking in such genres as blues, pop, and progressive rock, the lads gelled musically in a way they had not done for a long time. George brought to the table two of the best songs of his career, with the glorious 'Something' and 'Here Comes the Sun', accepted as one of the

best songs on the album, the results of his ever more mature songwriting skills. Sinatra remarked that 'Something' was "the greatest love song ever written". No one could dispute George's talent now. Lennon and McCartney provided a veritable cascade of songs, with everyone working in harmony. Even Ringo added 'Octopus's Garden', that softly wafted its undercurrent of longing for safety and happiness under the sea. All just as Paul had wanted.

But it was nothing more than a hologram of harmony. Paul was taken in by the illusion of reality, but its dramatic collapse hit him hard. Just as he was trying to persuade the others to play live in some small venues, John lit the fuse; he was leaving the group. The announcement was being delayed only because Klein was on the edge

of a phenomenal agreement dealing with their record royalties. Klein had soon squeezed from Capitol Records an unparalleled $0.69 for each Beatles album sold in America.

The cork popped from the bottle and an angry confrontation arose, with John, Paul and George hurling accusations at one another, until Paul urged them to calm down, convincing himself that John would not really leave.

This latest news, maliciously lining up behind his distrust of Klein, overwhelmed Paul, and he retreated into silence on his farm in Scotland with Linda and their first baby together, Mary.

Six days after John's news, on the 26th of September, Abbey Road, was released – its iconic sleeve depicting the four Liverpudlians striding across a zebra crossing outside

Abbey Road Studios was to become one of the most imitated images in the world. The reviews were mixed; "Round-the-clock production of disposable music effects" was one comment, but it went straight to number one in the UK and the US and several other countries.

John's continuing Peace Crusade made more headlines, however, and he was named man of the year by Rolling Stone magazine.e.

The split in the edifice was finally causing the building to crumble.

Paul and John didn't speak for almost six months.

TA-RA THEN LAD

When the final session for 'Let it Be' was over, not even Paul could face editing the mass of confused takes. Eventually, he consented to allow Phil 'Wall of Sound' Spector to be brought in to polish the mixes. What emerged was a halfway house of an album, partly with the studio noises left in and partly with the Spector touch added. Perhaps the moment when Paul gave up on the Beatles was when he heard 'The Long and Winding Road' suffocated under a choir and violins.

Licking his wounds, he concentrated instead on his own album that he had put together in Scotland by himself with help from Linda. It would be called simply McCartney.

In March 1970, Paul finally rang John with the news that he was putting out an album and that he, too, was quitting the group. The state of mind that Paul was in can be seen from an incident that occurred when Ringo popped around to Paul's house to say that the McCartney album would have to be postponed because Let It Be was about to be released. Paul went "completely out of control" according to Ringo, and told him to put his coat on and get out. It says a lot for Ringo's character that he understood what was going on, and despite the personal abuse, then persuaded everybody to postpone the release of 'Let it Be' in favour of Paul's album.

Ringo also had an album ready to go; Sentimental Journey was released on the 27th of March 1970 to what, at best, can be called tepid reviews. It was an album of old standards such a 'Night and Day', 'Whispering Grass (Don't Tell the Trees)' or 'Bye Bye Blackbird', arranged by a variety of people including Maurice Gibb, John Dankworth and Paul McCartney.

Ringo's marriage was now sinking fast; his infidelity and increasing alcoholism had taken their toll – "Years I've lost, absolute years … I've no idea what happened. I lived in a blackout", Ringo would confess years later. He and Maureen would eventually divorce in 1975 once his affair with the American model Nancy Andrews became public.

Soon after, on the 17th of April, McCartney the album hit the streets. But what happened immediately upon its release caused a furore.

"Do you foresee a time when Lennon and McCartney become an active songwriting partnership again?"

"No."

Those were Paul's words in a mock interview that was included with the album. He had officially given the word that The Beatles were no more.

Bitterly galled that John had been the one to break up the group, Paul had announced to the world that he, in fact, had been the one who had decided to walk out first. John, having kept his word not to announce his departure before the Beatle's final album was released, was incensed by Paul's egotism and underhand behaviour.

78

Phil Spector with George Harrison

80

an intimate bioscopic experience with

THE BEATLES

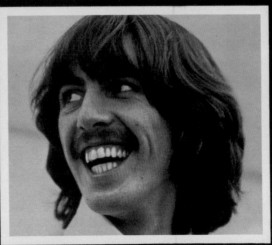

APPLE

An abkco managed company

presents

"Let it be"

ORIGI
AVAI

Poster for the Apple Corps movie 'Let It Be'

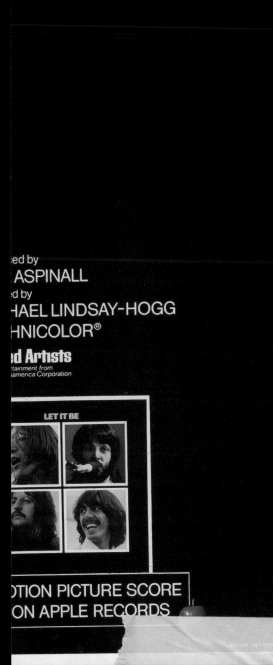

The news was also taken badly outside the band's world, and the album received an unfavourable response from the majority of music critics, although 'Maybe I'm Amazed' was praised. The album went to number 1 in the US and number 2 in Britain. The reviews were brutal, even personal; "… sheer banality"; "He seems to believe that anything that comes into his head is worth having. And he's wrong." "… the only Beatle who has stagnated as a human being". "Arrogant." "Second rate."

Sobering reading that must have pleased John.

So now there was nothing left except one wraith-like and orphaned musical child left to bring into the world.

Released in May 1970, Let it Be went to the top of the charts in the UK and the US and the singles of 'Let It Be' and 'The Long and Winding Road' reached number one in the US, though critics were generally disappointed. NME wrote: "If the new Beatles' soundtrack is to be their last then it will stand as a cheapskate epitaph, a cardboard tombstone, a sad and tatty end to a musical fusion which wiped clean and drew again the face of pop."

McCartney tried in vain to have the Spector version of 'The Long and Winding Road' stopped or changed, and George Martin said with a touch of bitterness that the credits should have read "Produced by George Martin, over-produced by Phil Spector".

The documentary that showed the group during the recording sessions for Let it Be was released on the 13th of May in New York and the 20th in the United Kingdom. Reviews were lukewarm. Its highlight was the session outdoors on the roof of the Apple building.

And that was it.

The Beatles would fade into legend, four youths frozen in time at the zenith of their musical creativity. The stratospheric comet that had been the Beatles had crossed the sky and faded into darkness.

And bitterness.

81

NOTHING IS ETERNAL

For George, the breakup released him from the stranglehold that John and Paul exercised on the Beatles' output.

In November 1970, like a shooting star, his triple album, All Things Must Pass, was released and powered up to no. 1 in the UK, the US, and all over the world as though to prove his point. Ringo was there to drum, Clapton was on guitar on what was considered to be the best solo album by any of the Beatles. George had finally come into the spotlight with all guns blazing.

"A major talent unleashed", said one critic.

'My Sweet Lord', said George.

The albums Living in the Material World, Thirty Three and 1/3 and Cloud Nine followed, also to great success.

In 1971, Paul succeeded in having The Beatles partnership placed in the hands of a receiver, therefore wrestling it from Klein's grasp. John, whilst writing 'Imagine', the best-selling single that he ever wrote, still resented Paul and he and his ex-bandmate threw barbed-wire grenades at one another through their songs. Paul released the album Ram with Linda, and fed up with the 'finger wagging' he felt was coming from the Lennon-Ono camp, gave John even more reason to feel aggrieved with the lines "Too many people preaching practices," and "You took your lucky break and broke it in two."

But Paul had probably been the worst affected of all the members of the band by the break up.

Not even Linda had been able to prevent him from falling into a personal black hole as he first watched his relationship with John deteriorate and then the group break up. But she did the next best thing. Paul became so depressed that days would be spent drinking whiskey in bed as he lost any sense of orientation to his life. "I nearly had a breakdown" was his comment about that time. So Linda patiently and with love, guided him out of his emotional crash-landing by reminding him of his artistic talents and encouraging and persuading him to go on with his songwriting and recording. Linda, the children and Argyllshire, Scotland, where they now spent months closeted away from all the madness, saved his sanity.

After Ram, Paul and Linda formed a new group called Wings, in which Linda played keyboards at Paul's insistence, and it would occupy them for the next ten years. It was successful and it kept Paul busy. Even he, however, confessed in an interview in 2016; "We were terrible. We knew Linda couldn't play, but she learned, and looking back on it, I'm really glad we did it..."

Apart from Paul writing the title song for the James Bond film Live and Let Die, it was only with their third album, Band on the Run in 1973, that they achieved commercial and critical success. Paul's 1977 hymn to his Scottish retreat, 'Mull of Kintyre' even spent nine weeks at the top

John Lennon backstage with Yoko Ono on BBC TV's Top Of The Pops, 11th February 1970

Apple & abkco

PRESENT

Sun. Eve., Aug. 1st, 8 PM

GEORGE HARRISON RAVI SHANKAR AND.........

For the benefit of the homeless children of Bengla Desh through UNICEF

AIR CONDITIONED
madison square garden
Pennsylvania Plaza, 7th Ave., 31st to 33rd Sts.

Tickets: $10, $7.50, $6.50, $5.50, $4.50

TICKETS ON SALE TOM'W (THURS.) AT
MADISON SQUARE GARDEN & OVER 100 TICKETRON BOX OFFICES
IN THE METROPOLITAN AREA INCLUDING:

A&S · B. ALTMAN (N.J.) · BAMBERGERS
CHASE MANHATTAN BANKS · GERTZ
GIMBELS · GRAND CENTRAL STATION
MACYS · SEARS

Also available in Baltimore, Boston, Philadelphia,
Pittsburgh, Washington, D.C. For the Ticketron
outlet nearest you, call (212) 644-4400.

TICKETRON

84

of the UK charts. By that time, Paul and Linda had added Stella, 1971, and James, 1977, to the family.

George and Ringo were still friends at least; Harrison, with enormous personal dedication, staged the Concert for Bangladesh in New York City in August 1971 with Ringo's help.

John and Yoko moved to America, initially to gain custody of Yoko's seven-year-old daughter, where John became even more radical, aligned himself to Malcom X, and espoused feminism. Nonetheless, his virulent jealousy of Yoko continued – whilst

Ringo Starr & George Harrison with Bob Dylan & Leon Russell during the Concert For Bangladesh, Madison Square Garden, New York

he had affairs. John and Yoko had many sessions with the Los Angeles therapist and 'Primal scream' theory advocate Arthur Janov. The problems persisted, however, even when they moved into the Dakota building just off Central Park in New York. Eventually, in 1973, Yoko had had enough and John was dispatched to the West Coast. To all intents and purposes they were both now single again.

In 1973, there was another ex-Beatle breakup; George Harrison, too, was seduced by the adoring women around him and his affairs led to his marriage to Pattie Boyd collapsing. In 1974, they went their separate ways with Pattie saying that "George used coke excessively, and I think it changed him ... it froze his emotions and hardened his heart". Pattie's new love was Eric Clapton, but this love triangle did not sour the friendship between the two guitarists.

This was also the year that George's American tour failed so badly that he never toured there again and it heralded a downturn in his artistic achievement. He retreated into the 120 rooms of his gothic mansion near Henley, south Oxfordshire. But not alone.

George had met the woman who would stay loyally by his side through all of the storms to come and the quirks of his character, the "bedrock" of his life, as she was described.

He had met Olivia Trinidad Arias at a party in 1974, and after many telephone calls the relationship blossomed, so George invited her to join his American tour. She moved into Harrison's mansion and they eventually married in June 1977. Their son Dhani was born on August 1, 1978 and the pair were excellent parents, keeping the limelight away from their son.

'Settled' lives for three of the Fab Four.

John and Yoko finally got back together, and on his 35th birthday, John became a father to Sean Ono Lennon. From then on, he devoted his life to his son, and the trio travelled and visited their many other properties. By 1978, the McCartneys and the Lennon Onos were even able to enjoy friendly evenings together.

"I was really grateful that we got it back together before he died. Because it would have been very difficult to deal with if ... well, it was very difficult anyway" Paul would say decades later.

John seemed to have mellowed in the intervening years; now he found a taste for playing music again; after all, he said, "Life begins at 40, so they promise". By 1980, his ideas had been formulated into an album; Double Fantasy, released in November 1980. The reviews were poor. John seemed undaunted.

Just before 11 PM on the 8th of December, John arrived back at Dakota building in his limousine, walked towards the entrance as Mark David Chapman called him from behind, saying "Mr. Lennon", and then shot him five times in the back.

85

ODEON HAMMERSMITH

M.A.M. presents

WINGS IN CONCERT

EVENING 8-30 p.m.

Saturday, 26th May, 1973

CIRCLE
£1·50

BLOCK
11

Seat
B 6

No ticket exchanged nor money refunded
THIS PORTION TO BE RETAINED

John managed to stagger into the Dakota entrance hall before collapsing. Rushed to hospital in a police car, he was pronounced dead just a few minutes after he arrived.

The dreams of Beatles' fans the world over came crashing down. The magical ride was over.

Wings, too, was doomed once Paul had been arrested for possession of marijuana in Japan and then deported after nine days in prison; the worst experience of many he had with the drug in his post Beatles' days with both he and Linda being arrested for possession.

And Ringo? A quiet life post Beatles? Well, yes and no. No one quite knew what might happen to the ever optimistic and happy Ringo. But it was those very qualities that enabled him to work with and for a host of music stars, so that his album output kept pace with the others for the first years after the breakup. Sentimental Journey was followed by the country-inspired Beaucoups of Blues, recorded with the famous Nashville session musician Pete Drake. Ringo also pursued a career as a film actor, appearing in several features; amongst them were That'll Be the Day in 1973, Ken Russell's Lisztomania in 1975 and a version of himself in McCartney's Give My Regards to Broad Street in 1984.

So Ringo, the loved and praised drummer who was the foundation stone on which The Beatles sound was built, mastered the split well, kept in touch with the other Beatles, and he and George even wrote a US no. 1 hit together; 'Photograph'. Neither did he lose touch with John, and he played on John and Yoko's albums John Lennon/ Plastic Ono Band and the Yoko Ono/Plastic Ono Band in 1970. Then came his successful debut rock album, Ringo, and also Goodnight Vienna, featuring Elton John, another success.

But as the seventies moved on, Ringo's drinking helped to remove his motivation and his career dwindled. He and his friend Keith Moon were members of The Hollywood Vampires drinking club. "Junkies dabbling in music" was how he described himself and Moon. Nonetheless, he continued to play with other musicians and to record throughout the next decades.

In February 1980, Ringo was starring in the film Caveman, when he met the actress Barbara Bach. They became a couple and married on the 27th of April, 1981 in a ceremony attended by Paul and Linda and George and Olivia.

But one aspect of the drummer's life and that of his wife reached worrying proportions later, as he and Barbara eventually realised. So during October and November 1988, both Ringo and Barbara attended a detox clinic in Tucson, Arizona, to try and dampen their desire to drink several bottles a day, each receiving a six-week treatment for alcoholism. It did the trick, and Ringo got his life back on track. Ringo Starr & His All-Starr Band was the result, and the band gave concerts all over the world, with Ringo joined on stage, in what had now become a Beatle tradition, by his wife.

George, meanwhile, had entered into the life of a film producer when he had invested money in the film The Life of Brian and founded a very successful production company, HandMade Films. Also, just as the other three Beatles had done, he had formed a band; he joined forces with Jeff Lynne, Roy Orbison, Bob Dylan and Tom Petty in 1988 under the name the Traveling Wilburys, to great success.

For the McCartney's, too, there would be many more pleasurable days; when Linda became successful in her own right launching a range of vegetarian frozen foods and recipes. And when Paul received a knighthood in 1997 in the Queen's Birthday Honours.

TONIGHT
Rain, 30-35

TOMORRO
Partial cleari

Details, Page

TV listin

86

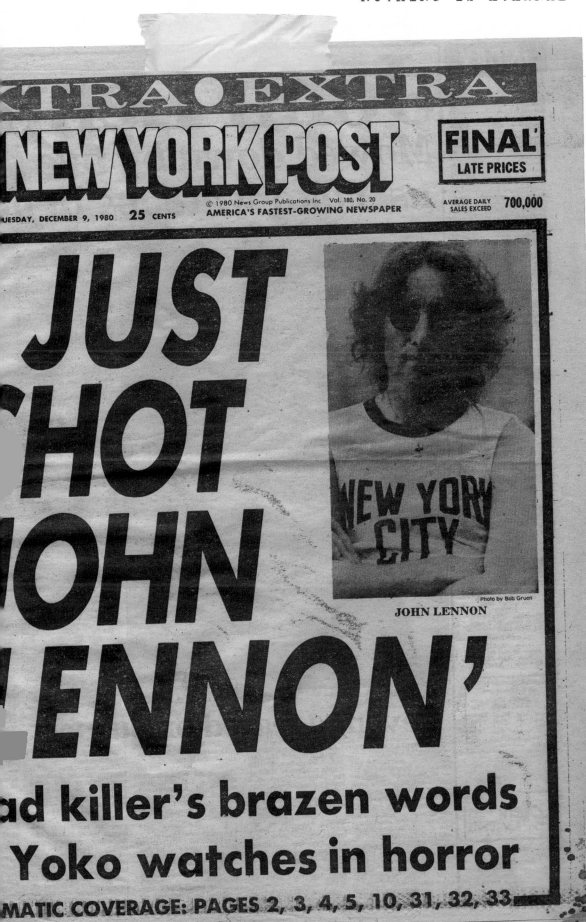

But the dark clouds were already overhead. There would be a price to pay for the largesse that had been bestowed upon them; each one of them would be affected.

Maureen, happily remarried to Isaac Tigrett of Hard Rock Café fame, and Ringo had remained good friends; he was beside her when the girl he once described as having such big and beautiful dark eyes that they hypnotised him, died in 1996; leukaemia had done its worst. Linda had been diagnosed with breast cancer in 1995. Paul knew that they had caught it too late. The disease spread rapidly and at the age of just 56, Linda died on the 17th of April 1998. 29 years of devoted marriage had been cruelly brought to an end. At least Linda had watched with pride her daughter Stella find success as a fashion designer. In 1997, more devastating news; George had been diagnosed with throat cancer. He had been a lifelong heavy smoker and this, he knew, was the result. An operation was successful and he was declared to be free of the disease.

Paul, the world's most eligible widower, was not one to be alone, and in early 1999 he was courting 32-year-old Heather Mills; a lady whose self-proclaimed biography seemed to throw up inconsistencies, and she was later described as "one of the shrewdest and most calculating women I've ever met". She was an antidote to Paul's bereavement, however, and despite a plethora of negative stories about her, even from her own family, they married on June the 11th 2002.

Paul continued to try and rewrite history by changing the 'Lennon–McCartney' credit on some of the Beatles songs to 'Paul McCartney and John Lennon', a sign that his ego was still in the driving seat of his actions. A sign, too, perhaps, that envy of John was undiminished even so many years after his death. In the attempt to cross from rock to 'legitimate art', Paul painted and wrote poems, which might best have been left unpainted and unwritten, accorded, as they were by author Phillip Norman, the words "amateur" and "pure embarrassment".

The gods of fortune were still not finished with the lesser gods they had created, and in 1999, one of George's worst nightmares became frighteningly real. On a "mission from God", a deluded Beatles' fan broke into George's home and stabbed him four times as they struggled with one another. Only Olivia, who set about the assailant with the base of a lamp and a poker, saved George, who was now bleeding profusely, from further injury until the police arrived.

"Aren't you glad you married a Mexican girl?", his friend Tom Petty said to him afterwards.

Cancerous cells were found in George's lungs in 2001. He knew that this time he would not win the battle, but in keeping with his life philosophies he refused to succumb mentally to the terrible disease and spend his last months in gloom. He reconciled with Paul and his sister Louise, and he and Dhani and Olivia were going to live "here and now", said his son, until George died on the 1st November to the sounds of Hare Krishna chants with Olivia and Dhani beside him.

88

Paul and Heather had a child together, Beatrice Mille, but the couple was divorced by 2008. Paul was already dating Nancy Shevall by 2007; they married in 2011.

And the hand of time moved on taking John's first wife, the "quiet, reserved and calm" Cynthia Lennon in 2015 – and then a man who has often been justifiably described as the "Fifth Beatle". George Martin, the bold, inquisitive and musically curious producer who gave the Beatles their beautiful arrangements and made tapestries that enhanced their early, raw, efforts, died in 2016. Despite John's, inevitably, disparaging remarks about him in 1972, Paul McCartney wrote of him that "If anyone earned the title of the Fifth Beatle it was George".

The band's success had been rooted in the talents of two competitive men, John and Paul, who could never be truly free of the bond that they had forged in the Liverpool musical hotbed of the 1950s. The competition sparked superb achievements but also resentments, and highlighted deep-seated incompatibilities. It was left to Paul to acknowledge the special relationship, and he did, many years after John's death.

"I couldn't have said that to him unless we were extremely drunk – I love you, man! – but you can put these emotions, these deeper and sometimes awkward truths, in a song."

A complex and thoughtful man, George had loved the Beatles but it was only when freed from Paul and John's power struggle that he had been able to expand creatively.

Yet what held true for George also held true for John and

Paul; without each other, as they all discovered but could never admit, with no one to chivvy them along, challenge them or censure them, they were not as good as they were together – but together they burst open the seams of pop music in a way no other band could match and showed the way for others to follow, using innovations in song structure and technique. They took studio production to new flamboyant and carefree heights that other bands strove to emulate.

The group that held the first five slots in the charts in one record-breaking week of April the 4th 1964, brought in the age of the singer-songwriter, making it the required norm for a singer to be able to compose. Not content with run-of-the-mill love songs, they moved on, exploring their own personal fault lines and those of the wider world, widening the scope of rock

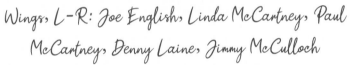
Wings, L-R: Joe English, Linda McCartney, Paul McCartney, Denny Laine, Jimmy McCulloch

89

music with harmonies and endless experimentation. Their influence on future generations of rock and pop musicians was incalculable.

As individuals, they defined the swinging sixties, challenging from the outset the corset of established behavioural norms with Liverpudlian wit and charm.

Winston Churchill once said that the world was made to be wooed and won by youth.

Without doubt, as they stormed through the world with grins on their faces, twinkles in their eyes and a witty riposte on their lips, The Beatles, George, John, Paul and Ringo, four cheeky young lads from Liverpool, certainly did that.

Ringo Starr and Marc Bolan during the making of the Apple Corps concert film 'Born to Boogie', 1972

20 THINGS YOU NEED TO KNOW ABOUT
THE BEATLES

THE QUARRY MEN

The glittering road that lay ahead for The Beatles was paved by the 50,000 plus skiffle bands popular in the UK in the mid-to late 1950s. Skiffle was an animated variation of American folk and country music – described as the 'punk' of its time because anyone capable of playing a few chords could form a band. In 1956 a 15-year-old John Lennon did just that – naming his creation The Quarry Men, inspired by the name of his school, Quarry Bank in Liverpool.

Originally a twosome, comprising John on guitar and a friend on washboard, the line up expanded by adding bass and drums to become a four-piece. The members were constantly changing but managed to make a name for themselves locally. In 1957 a 15-year-old skiffle fan called Paul McCartney. managed to wangle an introduction through a mutual friend and his knowledge of rock 'n' roll and guitars impressed John Lennon enough that he offered him a permanent place in the group. This new line up quickly proved its worth and made a big impact – including more rock 'n' roll in its sets. It wasn't long before the band was booked to appear in Hamburg.

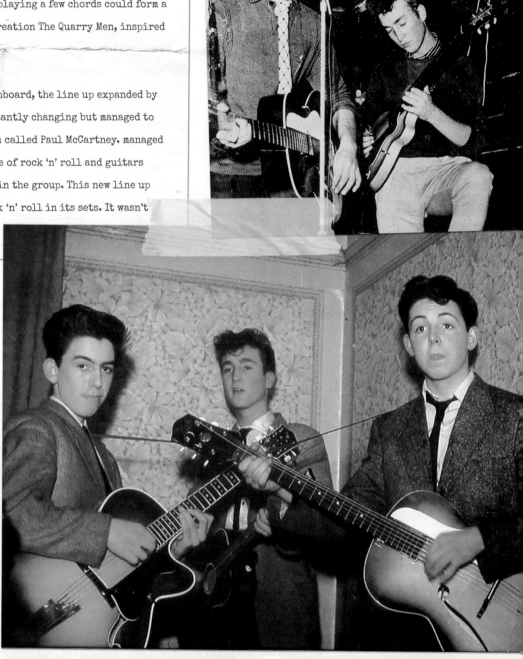

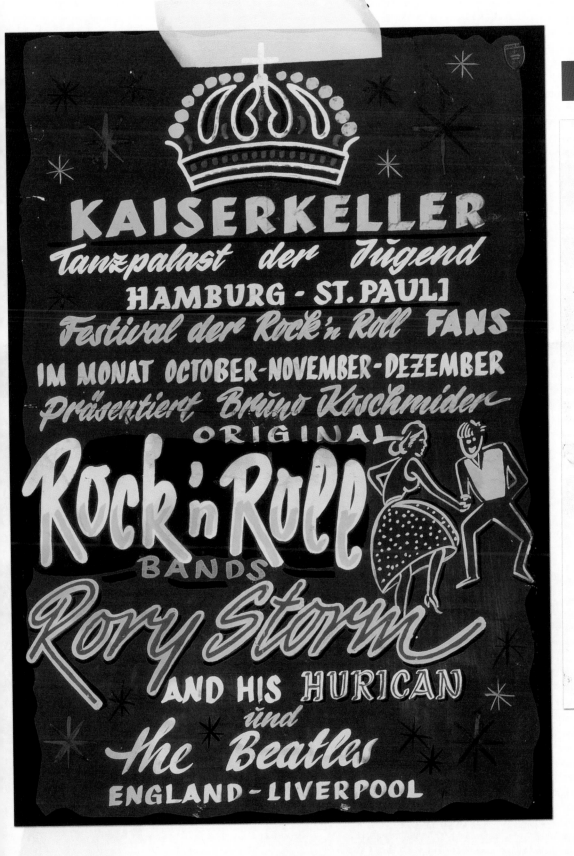

KAISERKELLER

Paul McCartney wasted no time in getting his friend George Harrison on board with The Quarry Men – although this meant upsetting the old order. After a few name changes, it was as 'The Beatles' that the first official line up of John, Paul, George, bass guitarist Stuart Sutcliffe and a new drummer Pete Best, began performing regularly at different clubs in Hamburg, Germany in August 1960. A popular haunt was the Kaiserkeller Club near the Reeperbahn.

The Beatles went on to work in Hamburg through to December 1962, improving their skills and reputation gig by gig. This chapter also got them noticed by industry professionals, giving them the chance to record their first single and to meet Brian Epstein, their first and most influential manager.

During their time in Hamburg, Sutcliffe – who had been instrumental in creating their famous 'mop top' hair cuts – decided to leave the group to continue his art studies, though sadly he was to die of a brain hemorrhage less than a year later, in April 1962. Epstein and the rest of the band decided to replace Best and bring in Ringo Starr in 1962, shortly after returning to the UK.

91

THE CAVERN CLUB

The Cavern Club is now famous the world over as the birthplace of The Beatles. It opened in a basement on Liverpool's Mathew Street in 1957 as a jazz club, but in line with the times, became a popular hangout for skiffle and rock 'n' roll groups.

The first appearance of The Beatles was at a lunchtime concert on 9 February 1961, for which they reportedly received £5. This debut was a success and led to four regular lunchtime slots a week, plus some weekend shows. Within weeks The Beatles were so popular that their appearances became ticket-only affairs and they performed at The Cavern nearly 300 times in the early 1960s. Their last performance was in August 1963. From then on – following their hit singles 'Please Please Me' and 'From Me To You' and with the accompanying 'Beatlemania' in full swing – it was impossible for the group to perform in such small venues.

92

THE BEATLES AT THE CAVERN

10 MATHEW STREET [OFF NORTH JOHN STREET]
LIVERPOOL [Telephone: CENtral 1591]

SATURDAY 3rd AUGUST 1963

ALSO ON THE SAME TERRIFIC PROGRAMME:

THE MERSEY BEATS

THE ESCORTS

THE ROAD RUNNERS

THE SAPPHIRES

JOHNNY RINGO & THE COLTS

SHOW STARTS AT 6 p.m. & FINISHES AT 11-30 p.m.

TICKET PRICE 9/6

The sale of which is strictly limited to Cavern Club Members only, who must produce their Membership Cards when purchasing the ticket and both ticket and Membership Card must be presented at the Club on the night. This rule will be strictly enforced.

OPERATION

'BigBeat'

TOWER BALLROOM

NEW BRIGHTON

Friday, 10TH Nov. 1961

7·30 P.M. to 1·0 A.M.

★ Rocking to Merseysides TOP 5 GROUPS

The Beatles
Rory Storm and the Hurricanes
Gerry & The Pacemakers
The Remo Four
Kingsize Taylor and the Dominoes

2 LICENSED BARS (until 11·30 P.M.) BUFFET

Special Late Transport (L,POOL · WIRRAL · CHESHIRE)

TICKETS 5!- from RUSHWORTHS · LEWIS'S
CRANES · STOTHERS
TOWER BALLROOM

GROWING FAME

With Ringo Starr and Brian Epstein as new drummer and manager respectively, The Beatles turned professional. George Martin came on board as producer and made a fantastic contribution to their recordings, style and development. Martin is among several people (including Epstein, Sutcliffe and Best) who are regularly listed as 'the fifth Beatle' – and he surely has a strong claim to the title. Building on their early success, Martin producing their first hit singles 'Love Me Do' and 'Please Please Me' during 1962/63.

Although they were already top of the bill at regional events, the venues they could fill were set to improve dramatically!

Concert poster for the Tower Ballroom Friday 10th November 1961.

I'M BUGS ABOUT THE BEATLES

I'M BUGS ABOUT the "BEATLES"

In 1963, the Beatles were unstoppable in their UK homeland. Their debut LP, 'Please Please Me', came out in March and held the number one spot for 30 weeks, followed by their megahit single 'She Loves You' in August. Their second album, 'With The Beatles', and hit single, 'I Want to Hold Your Hand,' followed that autumn. By the end of the year, the Beatles had five singles in Britain's Top 20, three of which hit number one. The frenzied fan phenomenon which became known as Beatlemania built and built throughout 1963 when teenage girls began screaming and crying while watching their performances. The noise of such collective hysteria mostly drowned out the music. Police escorts were necessary as fans began variously fainting or chasing the band at public appearances.

1964

Beginning the British Invasion of America

February 1964 saw The Beatles, by now affectionately nicknamed 'the Fab Four', made their first transatlantic trip to America to appear live on TV on The Ed Sullivan Show, drawing an audience of some 73 million Americans. Their arrival at John F Kennedy Airport in New York City was headline news. Despite the fact they arrived with a number one hit 'I Want To Hold Your Hand', to their name, the US music market was notoriously difficult to crack and no-one was sure what the interest would be. But they were greeted by a screaming crowd estimated to be 5,000 strong – the omens were good.

They performed their first US concert, a show at Washington Coliseum, Washington, D.C. a few days later on Feb 11, followed the next day by a show at Carnegie Hall in New York. They rounded off the whistle stop tour with another performance on the Ed Sullivan show before returning to the UK on 22 February 1964. What came to be known as The British Invasion had begun.

94

American Beatles fans wave Union Jacks at the Washington Coliseum

SEC. 16 H 3
ROW SEAT

WASHINGTON COLISEUM
3rd & M STS. N.E.. WASHINGTON, D.C.

ARCUS-SIMPLEX-BROWN INC. N.Y.C.

TUE. EVE.
FEB. 11

THE BEATLES

ARENA

1964
8:00 P.M.

Est. Price $3.73
Fed. Tax .27 Total **$4.00**

THE BEATLES

62 B 11 BEHIND STAGE

AUGUST **21**

1964

GLOBE TICKET CO., TACOMA

GOOD ONLY
FRI. EVE.
AUGUST

Enter Tunnel

62 B 11 SEC. ROW 12A SEAT BEHIND STAGE

FRI. EVE. – 8:00 P.M.

SEATTLE CENTER
COLISEUM

EST. PR. $2.75
FED. TAX .17 **$3.00**
CITY TAX .08

SUBJECT TO INSTALLATION
NO REFUNDS — NO EXCHANGES

FRI. EVE.
AUGUST **21**

1964

MORE AMERICAN SUCCESS

As part of their spring/summer 1964 world tour, the Beatles made a triumphant return to the United States in August. The gigs included the band's first appearance at the Hollywood Bowl in Los Angeles – the 18,700 tickets selling out months in advance. The set included 'Things We Said Today', 'Roll Over Beethoven', 'Boys', 'All My Loving', 'She Loves You' and 'Long Tall Sally' – all of which are included on the 1977 album, 'The Beatles at the Hollywood Bowl'. The other tracks on this album came from two subsequent concerts at this venue. Capitol Records recorded the Hollywood Bowl shows with the idea of producing a live album, but the sound quality of the recordings were disappointing and deemed unsuitable for commercial release. The Beatles were among the few major recording artists of the 1960s not to have issued a live album at the time.

US TOUR 1964

The Beatles returned to America in August 1964 for a month-long tour of 30 concerts in 23 cities, starting in San Francisco and ending in New York. Every event received massive coverage from local press and was attended by anything from 10,000 to 20,000 fans, whose screaming largely drowned out the music. The band earned over a million dollars in ticket income, with sales of records and merchandise receiving a further boost.

95

A HARD DAY'S NIGHT

Days after returning to England from their triumphant live appearances in America, John, Paul, George and Ringo began filming their first film, A Hard Day's Night. Pop and show business were more closely linked in those days so it wasn't as random a move as it may now appear. It was a musical comedy, mock documentary-style film portraying 36 hours in the lives of the Fab Four, during which they board a train en route to a live television appearance, accompanied by their 'manager' and Paul's 'grandfather' – while mayhem ensues.

As well as the title track, the UK soundtrack included 'And I love her', 'Tell Me Why' 'Can't Buy Me Love' and 'When I Get Home'. With all 13 tracks written by Lennon and McCartney, this is the only Beatles album comprising entirely Lennon-McCartney songs and demonstrates their developing strength as songwriters as they chose new, less chirpy and more reflective themes.

CONQUERING THE WORLD

The Beatles merry-go-round span even faster as they embarked on tours around the world, always to the same screaming reception inside and outside the concerts and hotels.

Whether it was Scandinavia, the Far East or Australia, the band never saw much more of the country than the inside of a hotel room, a dressing room, a limousine. Their one and only trip to Australia would have stood out however, with drummer Jimmy Nicol standing in for Ringo who had tonsillitis. The Beatles arrived in Sydney in June 1964, as the biggest band in the world greeted by one of the biggest ever crowds – 300,000 people strong.

Police hold back Beatles fans as Ringo Starr and Brian Epstein arrive at Sydney airport. The pair missed the early part of the Australian tour because Ringo had his tonsils out, 14 June 1964

CELEBRITY

Such was their celebrity by 1965 that The Beatles were a must on every guest list. Here John and Ringo are pictured with their then wives Cynthia, centre left, and Maureen, at the premiere of 1965 film 'The Knack' on June 3. Later that month John and Ringo, together with Paul and George of course, were awarded MBEs in the Queen's Birthday Honours. John originally seemed pleased, saying; 'Lots of people who complained about us receiving the MBE [status] received theirs for heroism in the war – for killing people ... We received ours for entertaining other people. I'd say we deserve ours more'. But four years later he was to return his medal as part of his ongoing peace protests.

1965 HELP!

The Beatles continued their film career with the making of Help! in 1965 with a quite ridiculous plot centred around a sacred ruby ring wanted by a religious cult which forces the Fab Four to go running through some exotic locations in Europe and the Bahamas.

The film came out on 29 July 1965. One review sums up many calling it; "...a failure, for as actors they are still nothing but Beatles, without enough characterisation – or even caricaturisation – to play anything but sight gags'. Nonetheless there were comparisons to the Marx Brothers and Ringo was singled out for particular praise.

But bad reviews didn't trouble the band's legions of fans. The film simply served, as had their first, as a vehicle for their songs. And what songs they were; 'Ticket to Ride', 'You've Got to Hide Your Love Away', 'Help' and one of their most covered and beautiful pop songs ever, 'Yesterday'. The accompanying 14-track album was released in August 1965 and reached number one in both the UK and the US.

Japanese poster for Richard Lester's 1965 musical film 'Help!' starring The Beatles

97

GAUMONT THEATRE
SHEFFIELD

ARTHUR HOWES in association with
BRIAN EPSTEIN presents
THE BEATLES SHOW
1st Performance at 6-15 p.m.
WEDNESDAY
DECEMBER 8
FRONT STALLS 15/-

A23

No ticket exchanged nor money refunded
THIS PORTION TO BE RETAINED

UK TOUR OF 1965

Fans in Liverpool,
queuing up outside for
the show. 6th December
1965 & Above, ticket
from Sheffield concert

98

As well as writing, recording and filming,
the band also had touring commitments to
fulfill. Their December 1965 concert tour
of the UK – which was to be their last –
saw them perform eight shows across nine
venues and coincided with the release of
the Rubber Soul album and double A-side
single 'Day Tripper/We Can Work it Out'.
Rubber Soul was a folk/rock album also
incorporating pop and soul elements.
The Beatles had matured as songwriters
and their musical tapestry was more
expressive, involving harmonium, sitars
and fuzz bass, with brighter tones for the
guitar. Two standout songs, McCartney's
'Michelle' and Lennon's 'Nowhere Man'
demonstrate the different approaches of
the songwriters and the widening rift
between them musically and personally.

1966 EUROPEAN AND WORLD TOURS

The Beatles' 1966 concert tour of America is notable for being
their fourth in the country and also the last commercial tour
they undertook. After this John, Paul, George and Ringo became
studio-based, focused on record production. It was a shame then
that the tour was plagued by controversy, particularly over one of
John's infamous remarks; 'We're more popular than Jesus now', which
resurfaced during the tour and provoked a huge backlash against
the band, including death threats. The concert in Candlestick Park
was their last commercial live performance.

REVOLVER

Released August 5 1966, the Revolver album represented The Beatles coming of age, demonstrating more sophisticated studio techniques and effects. Also, as Ringo has recalled, '...I think the drugs were kicking in a little more heavily on this album. I don't think we were on anything major yet, just the old usual– the grass and the acid.'

This album shows the band moving in a different direction, their themes including death, dreams and metaphysical transcendence. Its tracks include 'Eleanor Rigby', 'For No One' and Here, There and Everywhere' – three of McCartney's best ever ballads – along with 'Good Day Sunshine', 'Got to Get You Into My Life' and 'Yellow Submarine'.

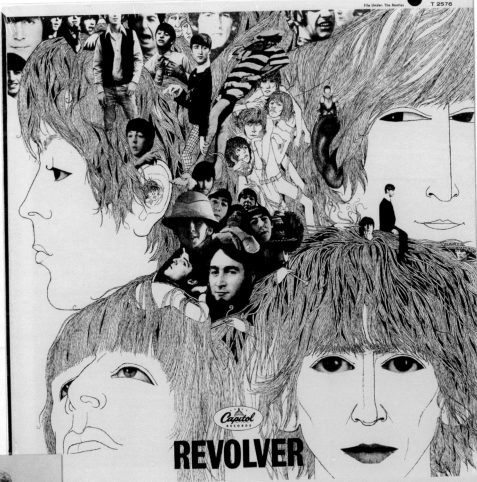

99

SGT. PEPPER

'Sgt. Pepper's Lonely Hearts Club Band' was The Beatles' eighth studio album and a huge artistic success. It hit the shops on 1 June 1967 and immediately topped the charts, remaining at number one in the UK for 27 weeks and in the US for 15 weeks.

Critics praised its innovations in music production, songwriting and graphic design, which linked pop music to legitimate art and gave musical form to 1960s counterculture. It won four American Grammy awards, including Album of the Year, making it the first rock LP to receive the honour. McCartney compositions dominated the track list, including treasures such as 'With a Little Help from My Friends', 'Lucy in the Sky with Diamonds', 'She's Leaving Home', and 'When I'm Sixty Four'.

MAGICAL MYSTERY
TV PRODUCTION

The Magical Mystery Tour was one of McCartney's ideas. Keen to use the plentiful material left over from Sgt. Pepper McCartney suggested the idea of touring around British seaside towns on a bus to see what 'surprises' could be elicited there. So in September 1967 a coach emblazoned with a Magical Mystery logo and carrying 43 assorted actors, journalists and novelty acts began its journey. There was no script, but also sadly no mystery, no magic and no humour. The show was panned after it was shown on television on Boxing Day 1967. However, once again, the soundtrack came to the rescue. It included one of the daftest Beatles songs of all time 'Hello, Goodbye' which went to number one in the UK and the US.

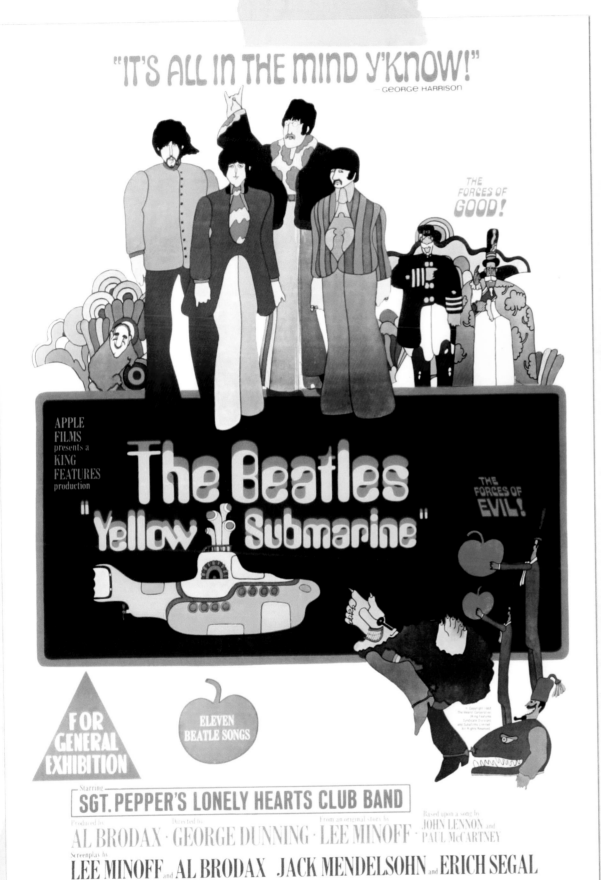

YELLOW SUBMARINE

This animated musical fantasy feature film, The Beatles' final commitment under their three-picture deal with United Artists, was a surprise hit when it was released to critical acclaim in July 1968. The Beatles put little effort into it; actors imitated their voices and the fab foursome created just four unreleased songs for the soundtrack including, 'Only A Northern Song' and 'It's Too Much'. The big hits from this album were 'Yellow Submarine' and 'All You Need is Love'.

The film itself included lush, wildly creative images, and has been credited as re-awakening interest in animation as a serious art form.

101

THE BEATLES

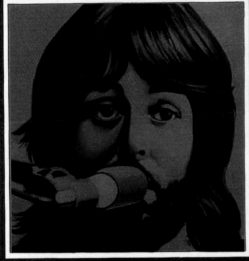

APPLE
AN ABKCO MANAGED COMPANY
presents
"Let it be"

PROD. **NELL ASPINALL** • REGIE **MICHAEL LINDSAY-HOGG** • **TECHNICOLOR** •

United Artists
Entertainment from Transamerica Corporation

IMPR. LICHTERT - Bruxelles 7

Let It Be was a feature film documenting the rehearsal and recording process for the 1970 album of the same name – their 12th and final studio album. It includes footage from their last performance together, playing on the roof of the Apple recording studios.

The film simply shot whatever 'action' was going on at the time; without commentary. None of the band were interviewed, but John, Paul, George and Ringo were shown working together in a cold and fraught atmosphere which, with the benefit of hindsight, illustrated the dynamic which would lead to their eventual break up. The film was shot during 1969 and begins by showing band rehearsals in a Twickenham sound studio, then the action moves to the Apple studio headquarters where recording begins. The climax of the film is footage of their impromptu rooftop concert above the recording studios, including performances of 'Get Back' and 'Don't Let Me Down'.

The Let It Be album released in May 1970 topped the charts in the UK and the US and the singles 'Let It Be' and 'The Long and Winding Road' reached number one in the States.

Belgian Let It Be poster, clockwise from top left: John Lennon, Paul McCartney, George Harrison, Ringo Starr, 1970

102

THE BEATLES' ROOFTOP CONCERT

The Beatles last live public concert on the rooftop of the band's Apple building in London's Saville Row created a minor sensation. Ringo Starr has since recalled that there was always a plan to play live somewhere during the recording of Let It Be, but the decision to play on the roof of their recording studio was taken just days before it happened on 30 January 1969. Together with Billy Preston on keyboards, the band played for 42 minutes – all filmed for the Let It Be documentary – performing five songs. Traffic came to a standstill as crowds realised what was happening. Police attended, asking the band to keep the noise down. Doubtless the noise and crowds would have multiplied had anyone known at the time that the band would never perform live again.

THE BEATLES DISCOGRAPHY

ALBUMS

TITLE	RELEASE DATE	CHART POSITION
My Bonnie	January 1962	
Please Please Me	22nd March 1963	UK 1
With the Beatles	22nd November 1963	UK 1
Les Beatles	November 1963	
Introducing the Beatles	10th January 1964	US 2
Meet the Beatles	20th January 1964	US 1
Twist and Shout	3rd February 1964	
The Beatles Second Album	10th April 1964	US 1
The Beatles' Long Tall Sally	11th May 1964	
A Hard Day's Night	26th June 1964	US 1
A Hard Day's Night	10th July 1964	UK 1
Something New	20th July 1964	US 2
Beatles for Sale	4th December 1964	UK 1
Beatles '65	15th December 1964	US 1
Beatles VI	14th June 1965	US 1
Help!	6th August 1965	UK 1
Help!	13th August 1965	US 1
Rubber Soul	3rd December 1965	UK 1
Rubber Soul	6th December 1965	US 1
Yesterday and Today	20th June 1966	US 1
Revolver	5th August 1966	UK 1
Revolver	8th August 1966	US 1
Sgt Pepper's Lonely Hearts Club Band	26th May 1967	UK 1 / US 1
Magical Mystery Tour	27th November 1967	UK 31 / US 1
The Beatles ("The White Album")	22nd November 1968	UK 1 / US 1
Yellow Submarine	17th January 1969	UK 3 / US 2
Abbey Road	26th September 1969	UK 1 / US 1
Let it Be	8th May 1970	UK 1 / US 1

104

THE BEATLES DISCOGRAPHY

LIVE ALBUMS

TITLE	RELEASE DATE	CHART POSITION
Live! At the Star Club in Hamburg, Germany; 1962	8th April 1977	US 11
The Beatles at the Hollywood Bowl	4th May 1977	UK 1 / US 2
First Live Recordings	1979	
Live at the BBC	30th November 1994	UK 1 / US 3
On Air – Live at the BBC Volume 2	11th of November 2013	UK 12 / US 7

COMPILATION ALBUMS

TITLE	RELEASE DATE	CHART POSITION
All the Beatles with Tony Sheridan and Their Guests	3rd February 1964	US 68
Jolly What!	26th February 1964	US 103
The Beatles Beat	15th April 1964	
Ain't She Sweet	5th October 1964	
The Beatles vs the Four Seasons	October 1964	US 142
The Beatle's Story	23rd November 1964	US 7
The Early Beatles	22nd March 1965	US 43
The Beatles	April 1965	
The Beatle's Greatest	18th June 1965	
The Beatles in Italy	13th July 1965	
Dans Leur 14 Plus Grand Succés	1st September 1965	
Los Beatles	19th November 1965	
Greatest Hits Volume 1	7th June 1966	
A Collection of Beatles Oldies	9th December 1966	
Greatest Hits Volume 2	February 1967	
The Beatles First	4th August 1967	
Hey Jude	26th February 1970	US 2
In the Beginning (Circa 1960)	4th May 1970	US 117
From Then to You	18th December 1970	
Por Siempre Beatles	8th October 1971	
All Essential Beatles	February 1972	
1962–1966 ("The Red Album")	19th April 1973	UK 3 / US 3
1967–1970 ("The Blue Album")	19th April 1973	UK 2 / US 1
Rock 'n' Roll Music	7th June 1976	UK 11 / US 2
Love Songs	21st October 1977	UK 7 / US 24
Rarities	2nd December 1978	UK 71
20 Golden Hits	1979	
Rarities	24th March 1980	US 21

105

TITLE	RELEASE DATE	CHART POSITION
The Beatles Ballads	24th March 1980	UK 17
Rock 'n' Roll Music Volume One	27th October 1980	
Rock 'n' Roll Music Volume Two	27th October 1980	
The Beatles 1967–1970	1980	
The Beatles	January 1982	
Real Music	22nd March 1982	UK 52 / US 19
20 Greatest Hits	11th October 1982	UK 10 / US 50
The Number Ones	1983	
The Early Tapes of the Beatles	10th December 1984	
Past Masters Volume One	7th March 1988	UK 49 / US 149
Past Masters Volume Two	7th March 1988	UK 46 / US 121
Past Masters Volume One & Two	24th October 1988	
Anthology 1	21st November 1995	UK 2 / US 1
Anthology 2	18th March 1996	UK 1 / US 1
Anthology 3	28th October 1996	UK 4 / US 1
Yellow Submarine Songtrack	13th September 1999	UK 8 / US 15
1	13th November 2000	UK 1 / US 1
Beatles Bop – Hamburg Days	6th November 2001	
Let it Be Naked	17th November 2003	UK 7 / US 5
Past Masters	9th September 2009	UK 31
Anthology Highlights	16th November 2010	
Tomorrow Never Knows	24th July 2012	UK 44 / US 24
I Saw Her Standing There	15th April 2013	
The Beatles Bootleg Recordings	17th December 2013	US 172

SINGLES

TITLE	RELEASE DATE	CHART POSITION
My Bonnie / The Saints	1961	UK 48 / US 26
Love Me Do / P.S I love You	1962	UK 17 / US 1
Please Please Me / Ask Me Why	1963	UK 2
From Me to You / Thank You Girl	1963	UK 1
She Loves You / I'll Get You	1963	UK 1 / US 1
I Want to Hold Your Hand / This Boy	1963	UK 1
Roll Over Beethoven / Please Mister Postman	1963	US 30
Misery / Ask Me Why	1963	
I Want to Hold Your Hand / I Saw Her Standing There	1963	US 1/100
Please Please Me / From Me to You	1964	US 3/41
Sweet Georgia Brown / Nobody's Child	1964	

THE BEATLES DISCOGRAPHY

TITLE	RELEASE DATE	CHART POSITION
All My Loving / This Boy	1964	US 31
Why / Cry for a Shadow	1964	
Twist and Shout / There's a Place	1964	US 1
Komm, gib mir deine hand / Sie liebt dich	1964	
Can't Buy Me Love / You Can't Do That	1964	UK 1 / US 1/77
Do You Want to Know a Secret? / Thank You Girl	1964	US 3/38
Sie liebt dich / I'll Get You	1964	
Ain't She Sweet / If You Love Me, Baby	1964	
Sweet Georgia Brown / Take Out Some Insurance on Me, Baby	1964	
Ain't She Sweet / Nobody's Child	1964	US 14
A Hard Day's Night / Things We Said Today	1964	UK 1
A Hard Day's Night / I Should Have Known Better	1964	US 1/43
I'll Cry Instead / I'm Happy Just to Dance	1964	US 22/91
And I Love Her / If I Fell	1964	US14/64
Matchbox / Slow Down	1964	US 17/34
I Feel Fine / She's a Woman	1964	UK 1 / US 1/8
If I Fell / Tell Me Why	1964	
Eight Days a Week / I Don't Want to Spoil the Party	1965	US 1/83
Ticket to Ride / Yes It Is	1965	US 1
Rock and Roll Music / I'm a Loser	1965	
No Reply / Rock and Roll Music	1965	
Help! / I'm Down	1965	UK 1 / US 1
Yesterday / Act Naturally	1965	US 1/28
I'll Follow the Sun / I Don't Want to Spoil the Party	1965	
Roll Over Beethoven / Misery	1965	
Boys / Kansas City, Hey, Hey, Hey	1965	US 73/75
We Can Work it Out / Day Tripper	1965	UK 1 / US 1/10
Michelle / Girl	1966	
Nowhere Man / What Goes On	1966	US 2
Paperback Writer / Rain	1966	UK 1/ US 1/31
Yellow Submarine / Eleanor Rigby	1966	UK 1/ US 1/12
Penny Lane / Strawberry Fields Forever	1967	UK 2 / US 1/10
All you Need is Love / Baby You're a rich Man	1967	UK 1/ US 1/60
Hello Goodbye / I am the Walrus	1967	UK 1/ US 1/46
Lady Madonna / The Inner Light	1968	UK 1 / US 2
Hey Jude / Revolution	1968	UK1 / US 1/11
Ob-La-Di, Ob-La-Da / While My Guitar Gently Weeps	1968	
Get Back / Don't Let Me Down	1969	UK 1 /US 1
The Ballad of John and Yoko / Old Brown Shoe	1969	UK 1 / US 10
Something / Come Together	1969	UK 4 / US 2/1
Let it Be / You Know My Name (Look Up the Number)	1970	UK 2 / US 1

TITLE	RELEASE DATE	CHART POSITION
The Long and Winding Road / For You Blue	1970	US 1/71
All Together Now / Hey Bulldog	1972	
Yesterday / I Should Have Known Better	1976	UK 8
Got to Get You into My Life / Helter Skelter	1976	US 3
Back in the USSR / Twist and Shout	1976	UK 19
Ob-La-Di, Ob-La-Da / Julia	1976	UK 19
Sgt Pepper's Lonely Hearts Club Band / With a Little Help From My Friends / A Day in the Life	1978	UK 63 / US 92
The Beatles Movie Medley / I'm Just Happy to Dance	1982	UK 10 /US 14
Baby It's You	1995	UK 7
Free as a Bird / Christmas Time (Is Here Again)	1995	UK 2
Real Love / Baby's Back in Town	1996	UK 4 / US 11

EPs

TITLE	RELEASE DATE	CHART POSITION
My Bonnie	12th July 1963	
Twist and Shout	12th July 1963	UK 1
The Beatles' Hits	6th September 1963	UK 1
The Beatles (No. 1)	1st November 1963	UK 2
All My Loving	7th February 1964	UK 1
Souvenir of Their Visit to America	23rd March 1964	
Four by the Beatles	11th May 1964	US 92
Requests	18th June 1964	
Long Tall Sally	19th June 1964	UK 1
The Beatles Again!	July 1964	
A Hard Day's Night No. 1	July 1964	
The Beatles No. 2	July 1964	
Extracts from the Film A Hard Day's Night	4th November 1964	UK 1
Extracts from the Film A Hard Day's Night	6th November 1964	UK 8
4 by the Beatles	1st February 1965	US 68
Beatles for Sale	6th April 1965	UK 1
Beatles for Sale No. 2	4th June 1965	UK 5
The Beatles Million Sellers	6th December 1965	UK 1
Yesterday	4th March 1966	UK 1
Nowhere Man	8th July 1966	UK 4
Magical Mystery Tour	8th December 1967	UK 2

109

THE BEATLES

FEB.

1

ARENA

Est. Price $3.73 Total $4.00

P.M.

1964

THE BEATLES

RINGO "RINGS" STARR

GAUMONT THEATRE

SHEFFIELD

ARTHUR HOWES in association with BRIAN EPSTEIN presents

THE BEATLES SHOW

1st Performance at 6-15 p.m.

WEDNESDAY

DECEMBER 8

FRONT STALLS 15

A23

nanged nor money refunded
ON TO BE RETAINED

LOWER GRANDSTAND

8 25 10

WHITE SOX PARK

35th and SHIELDS

AUG. 20

FRIDAY 8:00 p.m.

THE BEATLES

1965

EST. PRICE 2.36 $2.50
FED. TAX .14

No Refunds — No Rain Date

BEATLES —

ARK STADIUM

W ORLEANS, LA.

Y EVENING 8:00 P.M.

ADMIT ONE

EST. PR. 4.32 TOTAL
FED. TAX .33 $5.00
WEL. TAX .22
C & S TAX .13

NDS FOR ANY REASON
TION OF SHOW.

GOOD ONLY WEDNESDAY EVE.
SEPTEMBER 16 1964

THE BEATLES CITY PARK STADIUM — NEW ORLEANS, LA.

23434

BOX 1041

HOLLYWOOD BOWL

2301 N. Highland Ave.

HOLLYWOOD   CALIFORNIA

AUG. 29

SAT. EVE. AUG. 29, 8:00 P.M.

KRLA and BOB EUBANKS Presents

"THE BEATLES"

1965

$5.00   PRICE $5.00

INDIANA STATE FAIR

STATE FAIRGROUNDS — Indianapolis, Ind.

Wm. F. Johnson, Pres.   Hal L. Royce Secy. — Mgr.
Richard O. Ristine, Commissioner of Agriculture

THE BEATLES

SEP. 3

THURSDAY 5:00 P.M. (EST)

SIDE MEZZANINE — $5.00

Est. Price 4.64 — Fed. Tax .36

1964

THE BEATLES

THE BEATLES

INDIANA STATE FAIR COLISEUM

GOOD ONLY THURSDAY AFT. SEP. 3

SIDE MEZZ.

SEC. 19 ROW G SEAT 12

AISLE-15

THE ARGUS TICKET CO. CHICAGO

95

1964

WINTER GARDENS

BOURNEMOUTH

SATURDAY

NOVEMBER 16

8.30 p.m.

STALLS 12/6

ARTHUR KIMBRELL PRESENTS
THE BEATLES

i 40 i 40

TICKETS CANNOT BE EXCHANGED OR TAKEN BACK
TO BE RETAINED

THE BEATLES AT THE CAVERN

10 MATHEW STREET [Off NORTH JOHN STREET]
LIVERPOOL [Telephone: CENtral 1591]

SATURDAY 3rd AUGUST

ALSO ON THE SAME TERRIFIC PROGRAMME:

THE MERSEY BEATS
THE ESCORTS
THE ROAD RUNNERS
THE SAPPHIRES
JOHNNY RINGO & THE COLTS

SHOW STARTS AT 6 p.m. & FINISHES AT 11-30 p.m.

TICKET PRICE 9/6

The sale of which is strictly limited to Cavern Club
Members only, who must produce their Membership Card
when purchasing the ticket and both ticket and Membership
Card must be presented at the Club on the night.
This rule will be strictly enforced.

MEMBER BEATLES FAN CLUB

ATLES S

FOR RELEASE ON APRIL 9

ease April 9 on EMI's PARLOPHONE label

TLES single

KET TO RIDE and YES IT IS

-McCartney compositions,
in THE BEATLES NEW FILM.

fastish number features
ng, with JOHN taking the lead.

is slow and in three-part harmony
with JOHN again taking

THE BEATLES

PAUL McCARTNEY
JOHN LENNON
GEORGE HARRISON
RINGO STARR

SEC. 42 Q ROW Q SEAT 2

UPPER RESERVED

SHEA STADIUM

FLUSHING, N.Y.

TUESDAY AUG. 23 1966 7:30 P.M.

SID BERNSTEIN, Presents

"THE BEATLES"

PRICE $5.75

PERFORMANCE HELD
RAIN OR SHINE

SID BERNSTEIN, Presents

NO REFUNDS - NO EX

SEC. 42 Q ROW Q

UPPER RESERVED $5.75

TUE. AUG. 23-1966-7

KYA RADIO 1260

WELCOMES

THE BEATLES

AT CANDLESTICK PARK - SAN FRANCISCO

MONDAY AUGUST 29, 1966 - 8:00 P.M.

NO REFUNDS

RINGO   JOHN   PAUL   GEORGE

I'M BUGS ABOUT the "BEATLES"